SOMEONE LIKE ME

An Unlikely Story
of Challenge and Triumph
over Cerebral Palsy

John W. Quinn

Published in the United States by
History Publishing Company
Palisades, New York

LCCN: 2010921778
ISBN-10: 1-933909-74-9
ISBN-13: 978-1-933909-74-5
SAN: 850-5942

Quinn, John W., 1962-
      Someone like me : an unlikely story of challenge and
triumph over cerebral palsy / John W. Quinn.
      p. cm.
      Includes index.
      LCCN 2010921778
      ISBN-13: 9781933909745
      ISBN-10: 1933909749

      1. Quinn, John W., 1962- 2. Cerebral palsied--
Biography. 3. United States. Navy--Officers--Biography.
4. Cerebral palsy--Biography.   I. Title.

      RC388.Q56 2010   362.196'836'0092
                                  QBI10-600039

Printed in the United States on acid-free paper

9 8 7 6 5 4 3 2 1

First Edition

To Phil Freeman

*For always putting the needs of others before
your own—I'm placing you first.*

"Some succeed because they are destined to, but most succeed because they are determined to."

—*Henry Van Dyke,*
American author, educator, and clergyman

CONTENTS

This book is written entirely from my own personal memory of places, events, people, and conversations. Although not word-for-word reenactments, this is every bit my story and not a work of fiction. Others may have a different slant on events, but these are mine. Several names of individuals have been changed in order to respect their privacy, but that's about it.

Introduction

I enjoy reading biographies and inspirational non-fiction. Looking for a book written by and about a disabled adult, I combed my local bookstore and library recently but found only two that came close to what I had in mind: *My Left Foot* by Christy Brown, and *Ten Things I Learned from Bill Porter* by Shelly Brady. I was disappointed by the lack of memoirs currently on the market written by adults coping with any disability, much less one specific to my condition—cerebral palsy.

Cerebral palsy is a handicap that currently affects over 750,000 people in the United States alone; most published material is primarily focused on infants and parenthood, e.g., "Your baby has cerebral palsy, now what?"

I found numerous medical journals describing the various types and causes of CP, and countless manuals explaining rights to possible legal action, but neither was what I wanted and needed.

I wrote *Someone Like Me: An Unlikely Story of Challenge and Triumph over Cerebral Palsy* to fill that void. I wanted to tell what it's like to have cerebral palsy as an adult. It is commonly known that the majority of people with CP go through years of physical therapy in their youth and typically, they suffer humiliation from being laughed at by schoolmates because of a limp or tremor. But it is generally not known what it is like to be an adult, facing such issues as getting and holding down a job, dating, and finding some measure of self worth. Some CP sufferers have symptoms much worse than I.

My sincere wish is that by sharing my story they may find some comforting commonality and be glad their voices are heard within these pages.

My story tells about the secret life I led. I now know that my family is not the only one to request that their child's condition be "kept a secret" because of the shame it would bring them. I know about secrets. I hid the fact of my cerebral palsy from Navy officials for twenty years. It feels good to finally tell the truth.

Although the book is filled with naval anecdotes and humor, this is not a military book. Nor is it only for the disabled reader. It is an inspirational memoir, full of nostalgic and quirky stories and dialogue garnered from life in a large Catholic family during the 1970s and 80s. My recollections of those years were enhanced by many interesting family discussions during the time spent working on this book, picking everyone's memory, going through thousands of photos, and reading through all the letters I wrote to my best friend Phil during my time at sea.

Someone Like Me wasn't easy to write. It was particularly difficult to retrace the times of my life that I'd rather forget. Some memories are still quite painful to re-live and others quite embarrassing. Additionally, I had never written anything for publication before. I didn't even know where to put the commas or the quotation marks when I began. Factor in the physical hardships someone with CP faces—sitting in a chair for hours with legs that tell me if I am going to write today or not, eyes that do not handle computer strain well, and my left-handed keyboard approach—then you begin to understand the challenges I faced.

I would like to acknowledge some of the people who were instrumental in helping me write this book. First of all, thanks to Don Bracken and everyone at History Publishing for believing in my story. My parents, Ed and Shirley, instilled in me the foundation for my success. I felt their love and support with every word I wrote. My sister, Susan, answered my countless e-mails and exhibited endless patience in helping me craft a well-built sentence. You do like words and it shows, Sis. My best friend, Phil, for never throwing anything away, including our friendship. Thanks for sending me those letters, pal. I also want to thank Pam and Barb for their wonderful editing advice, my hard-working agent, Claire Gerus, publicist Lynn Wiese-Sneyd, and the many friends who read draft after draft. To the dedicated men and women of the United States Armed Services—thanks for standing the watch.

And most of all, thanks to my readers… for letting me share the truth.

1

Don't Send Me Home

"Oh, no!" I groaned, hearing the military doctor give an order I knew I could not follow.

"One last exercise before you all become property of Uncle Sam. Everybody, get ready to do the duck walk!" he had barked. My mind raced as my pulse quickened. *What the hell was a duck walk?*

I was moments away from completing my military entrance examination. All that was left was one last stupid-sounding thing and my dream of joining the Navy would be fulfilled.

I had been stuck in downtown Detroit, getting my physical, since eight that morning. Blood had been drawn, eyes and ears checked. I'd peed into a cup, turned my head and coughed. Everything had gone smoothly.

It was now four in the afternoon and exhaustion had settled deeply into every muscle and bone in my body. *Let's just finish this up and get me sworn into the Navy. Then, I can go home and share the news with my family.* My mom was planning to make one of my favorite meals to celebrate: meatballs and gravy.

Just one last exercise.

"Let me show you how to do the duck walk," the doctor told us. "And I want it done in precisely this manner. No cheating allowed."

His keys jingled in his pocket while he hitched up his pant legs and crouched down on the ground, his white lab coat puddling around his feet. He resembled a major league catcher with his stony expression and arms out in front.

"I want you all to stay in this crouch and hold it until we have a chance to come around and take a look. Then I want you to walk, while remaining in the squat position with your arms straight out. You'll look like a duck out of water."

The physician demonstrated how to execute what he wanted done. A few guys quacked. My heart sank, followed quickly by my stomach. *You can do this, no big deal.* But I knew better.

"Ready—begin," said the doc.

I looked around at the fifty or so other guys who were taking the induction physical with me. Stripped to our boxers, we'd been herded like cattle from one room to the next for most of the day. The entire process had been a long, slow grind for everyone. I watched to see how the other enlistees were doing this simple movement. They made it look easy. It was as if the room were suddenly filled with a bunch of Johnny Bench All-Stars, ready to receive the first pitch of the World Series. The other enlistees were so comfortable that some flashed signs to an imaginary pitcher, one finger for a fastball and two for a curve. I was the last to get down on the ice-cold floor in my catcher's squat. Pain immediately shot up from my hips and my whole body started to shake uncontrollably.

Focus, just focus, I yelled into my brain, trying to make my limbs work.

"Okay, now stretch both your arms straight out in front of you, and hold that position as we come through and look," the doctor hollered. The guy meant business.

I tried to stick my arms out and fell over.

The doctors saw me collapse and headed in my direction. I quickly gathered myself and tried again, this time keeping my left hand on the floor for balance. I prayed they didn't notice. Sweat rolled off my body and my muscles strained with every second.

"Both hands out, son, let's see it," the doctor snapped, hovering over me.

I lifted my left hand off the floor, my face a picture of determination and fear. I fell again. The guy to my right chuckled and tapped the kid in front of him, pointing. They both laughed and the whole room joined in, as I scrambled to get up. The doctor wrote something on a clipboard file he was carrying. He was not laughing.

Only a couple of seconds had passed since I fell, but it felt like hours.

"Son, get out of line. Everyone else, stand up and stretch out your legs. Get over to the locker room, put your clothes back on quickly and step into the induction room. In a few minutes, you will raise your right hand and embark on your new life in the military. Let me be the first to offer my congratulations. Well done!" he said.

A cheer went up throughout the crowd. Guys were slapping each other on the back and giving out high fives. Everyone was smiling, everyone but the doc and me.

"You, come with me," said the doctor through the din of celebration.

As the passing candidates headed off to get into their civilian clothes, I, still in my boxers, was directed to a quiet corner and was quickly surrounded by three physicians.

"Stand up straight and look forward."

I did as I was told, hearing the voice of my mom. I was scared. My legs shook and trembled. The doctors circled, examining my body very closely. I heard the scratch of a pen on a metal clipboard. "Is that as straight as you can stand?"

"Yes, it is." The words came out as a squeak.

"Put your legs together." I matched them up as best I could while one doctor examined my lower limbs.

"Geez," I heard him say under his breath.

Another looked at my left shoulder blade. "Have you ever separated your shoulder?"

"No," I stated with all the conviction I could muster.

"Really?" the doc looked at me. "Does your back hurt you?"

"No, I feel fine."

"What about your hips? Were you ever in a car wreck?"

"Never."

One doctor called a colleague over. "Hey, Jim, look at this." He ran his thumb down the length of my spine. I shivered. "What is wrong with you, boy?"

"Nothing's the matter with me," I lied, looking the man square in the eye.

He took a step back and nodded his head. "Okay, if there's nothing wrong with you, get down on your haunches and put your arms out straight."

By then, the examination room was empty. It was just the three doctors and me. I got down in a squatting position, and right away my legs started to quiver.

I fell over.

"Nothing wrong with you, huh?" The three physicians chuckled.

I looked up from the green tile floor and set my jaw. *How dare they laugh*! "Give me one last chance, I can do this," I insisted.

"No, get up and put your clothes on. We've wasted enough time here. I'll meet with your recruiter and he will send you home."

Send you home. Those three small words sealed my fate. I turned back to the first doctor for confirmation.

"Son, I really don't know what is wrong with you, but you have a spine the shape of a pretzel. You cannot stand up straight, your legs are as bowed out as anyone I've ever seen and your hips are not aligned correctly. You are pigeon-toed. Your left shoulder is protruding forward, and on top of that, at six feet, one inch and 128 pounds, you're about twenty pounds under military weight standards. Go home and go to college. Get a job on the assembly line. Uncle Sam can't use someone like you."

Someone like me.

I had to laugh. Sure, there *was* something wrong with me. A secret only my family and closest friend knew about. A secret that I would keep deeply buried for the next 25 years.

I had been born with cerebral palsy.

I did not tell my recruiters about my handicap because I knew they would never allow me to enlist. And I wasn't going to tell the military doctors. As I slowly reached into my locker and put my clothes on, I could hear guys starting the enlistment oath...

"To support and defend the Constitution of the United States..."

The sound of their voices burned my ears. I was filled with jealousy and anger. I should be in that room, standing proudly with my chest puffed out, ready to serve my country.

"Against all enemies, foreign and domestic..."

I made a silent vow to myself. *I will be back.*

Next time, I would pass the physical and become a sailor.

"So help me God."

2

A Condition Called Cerebral Palsy

I have cerebral palsy. It feels good to admit that today, after all these years. How was I able to hide this fact? It wasn't easy.

According to the United Cerebral Palsy national web site, "cerebral" refers to the brain, and "palsy" to muscle weakness/poor control. Cerebral palsy itself is not progressive: the brain damage does not get worse. It is neither communicable nor is it a disease.

Cerebral palsy is instead a term used to describe a group of chronic conditions affecting body movement and muscle coordination. It's caused by damage to one or more specific areas of the brain—usually during fetal development or shortly after birth, or even from an injury during infancy. Thus, these disorders are not caused by problems in the muscles or nerves themselves. Instead, faulty development or damage to motor areas in the brain disrupts the brain's ability to adequately control movement and posture.

In short, my brain does not communicate well with my body, particularly my muscles.

More than 764,000 children and adults in the United States manifest one or more of the symptoms of cerebral palsy. A common trait includes muscle spasticity—sudden, involuntary muscle spasms. This uncontrolled movement or tremor is typically the result of poor muscle tone as well as rigidity, and since the brain is not always in charge when you have cerebral palsy, legs and arms can sometimes take on a life of their own.

I struggle with this still, especially when I am tired or nervous. And the shaking during my duck walk attempt at the recruitment center that day was only one symptom of many.

The rigidity I experience is continuous. I don't even notice it anymore. I've had people who know about my condition ask me if I'm in pain, and my answer is Zen-like—if pain is constant, is it even pain? Or is it merely my normal state of being?

This perpetual tension also makes my muscles work twice as hard, resulting in my body becoming fatigued easily. When muscles are working overtime at being tight and rigid, they don't have much energy to spare. Most CP sufferers exhibit moderate to severe musculature weakness.

Cerebral palsy can also affect skeletal development. Many muscles work in opposition, such as the ones in the legs. When one muscle in the pair tightens up so rigidly that it's almost paralyzed, as in a child with cerebral palsy, the bones that these muscles are attached to may not grow properly. The result is often skeletal abnormalities such as one leg longer than the other, one shoulder higher, and a misalignment of hips and spine.

In my case, the rigidity in the muscles supporting my thigh bones caused an inward twisting of hips, thighs, and knees. As I grew, I became pigeon-toed and bow-legged, with a scissor-like shuffling gait.

As a child, I had eyes that would wander independently of one another. Kids in school would point at me and laugh. When I spoke, I talked to the ground instead of the other person, embarrassed and ashamed of my appearance.

My eye condition also made reading and learning difficult. Many children with cerebral palsy have a tough time in mainstream classes. This is usually due to mental retardation resulting from the injury that caused the CP, or possibly vision defects such as mine.

To help correct my eyesight, I was prescribed thick, heavy glasses to wear during the day. Boy, were they ugly! I'm sure those glasses helped me learn to read and write, but they did nothing for my popularity or self-esteem. While everyone else played kick ball, I stayed close to the school building, not wanting to participate in

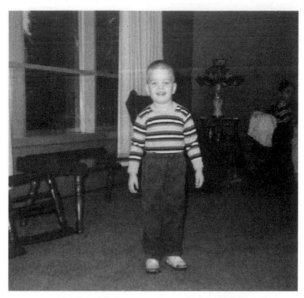

Wearing my corrective shoes, 1965

any physical activity. I was teased, shamed, and forced to grow a thick skin at a very early age.

I also had to wear a patch to cover my eye at night. The patch was placed over my "stronger" right eye, which forced my "weaker" left eye to focus and tighten up the muscles that controlled eye movement.

Of course, as a kid I couldn't really comprehend the medical reasoning behind this protocol; all I knew was that I hated my wandering eyes and the daily patch regimen. I detested my glasses and clunky orthopedic shoes too. They made me different and I didn't like it.

My parents were apparently in denial back then and never openly discussed the fact that I had cerebral palsy. Not once did they sit me down in a chair and say, "John, you have a physical condition called cerebral palsy and here's what we know about it." Because of this, I did zero research on CP until I was in my 20s. What caused it? Will it get worse? Will it get better? What can I do to help myself? Growing up, I didn't think to ask. I just accepted it.

Many years later I asked Mom about the general lack of discussion regarding my diagnosis. We were drinking iced tea and relaxing in her kitchen. My father had passed away a few years earlier. She explained that Dad had intentionally set the stage when I was young, not by denying or ignoring my symptoms, but by "choosing to make a decision based on a parent's concern for the future of his child."

"I'll tell you something that was very important to your father," she said. "Your dad never wanted the fact that you had cerebral palsy noted on any of your medical records. He was very clear to the doctors at Children's Hospital about this."

"Why was that, Mom?"

"Because he didn't want you to be labeled handicapped or disabled as you got older, like your sister Kathy."

"But Mom, I *was* handicapped."

"Not to your father and me. In fact, John," she'd said, leaning back in her chair and warming up to the story, "I can clearly picture the meeting in 1967 where we first learned of your condition. Dad and I were seated around a large conference table at Children's Hospital with a bunch of doctors in their white coats…"

"Thank you for coming, Mr. and Mrs. Quinn. Dr. Jennings, your family doctor, speaks highly of the Quinn household, especially this wonderful little boy, John."

"Thanks for taking the time here, everyone," Dad said as he stood for introductions all around. "For those who don't know me, my name is Ed and this is my wife, Shirley."

Although of slight build, Dad was an imposing man nonetheless. He had ink-black hair combed straight back, a firm jaw line, and deep set brown eyes that could drill you to the wall from across a crowded room. By contrast, with her blond curls and quiet demeanor, Mom served as the perfect foil to Dad's intimidating presence. She even stood a few inches shorter, almost by design. They shared a weary, worried look as Dad sat down and the meeting commenced.

"Ed, Shirley, the reason that we are here today is to give you the results of the testing that was conducted on John last month."

"All we want is to finally get a straight answer as to what is wrong with our boy," Dad said, staring at the far corner of the room where I was scribbling in a coloring book.

"I know that this process has been frustrating and difficult for you and your wife, and we appreciate your patience. Hopefully we can address many of your questions today. Shirley, for the benefit of everyone at this table, can you please give us a rundown of your concerns?"

"Sure. Well, Johnny is four and a half years old and we are ready to place him into kindergarten next fall."

"But you have some reservations?"

"Yes. For one, he is not very coordinated."

"What do you mean, Shirley?"

"Well, he didn't learn to walk with any confidence until a year or so ago."

"I understand that he was slow in his motor development?"

"Yes, he didn't begin to pull himself up on his feet until he was about 15 months old. I'd say Johnny was two years old when he began walking more than crawling."

"I see. What about playing with other children, his brothers and sisters? How does he get along?"

"Socially, he gets along great. He is a smiling, happy little boy."

"But physically?"

"Physically, he struggles," said my dad.

"In what way, Ed?"

"He cannot run very well and has a hard time keeping up with everyone. The same with climbing stairs, he has to hold onto the banister with both hands and almost pull himself up. Hell, he can't even pull a wagon without tripping over his feet. It's painful to watch."

"Sounds like you have a tough son there."

"Yes, John is plenty stubborn and very determined. I can see that already. But I am concerned about him always getting picked on or left behind as he goes through life. Even now, as a kid, I watch him play in the neighborhood and he is consistently last across the finish line."

"And this bothers you?"

"Hell yes, it does," said my father. "We all know how difficult life is, and I can just imagine how much tougher it becomes for someone like John. Is he going to come in last for the rest of his life? Can you answer that for me, Doc?"

"No, I can't, Mr. Quinn. Only time will tell how your son deals with the challenges he will face. I know you and Shirley will support him emotionally, but our focus right now is on identifying and treating his physical limitations."

"I'm also very worried about his eyes," my mom said. "They don't appear to be straight."

The physician nodded. "Our testing did indicate vision disturbances, which are part of the larger diagnostic picture. We'll give you the results of our testing now and I'm sure you will have some questions."

Mom and Dad sat still, their eyes focused on the doctor who had picked up a file from the table, and with slow precision was turning the cover.

"Our testing revealed that John has cerebral palsy."

It got quiet in the conference room.

"Do you know what that is?"

Mom and Dad in unison shook their heads.

The doctor explained that at some point in my fetal development, my brain had been damaged.

Mom pulled a crumpled tissue out of her huge purse, wiped her eyes and asked, "Why?"

"Causes vary, and are often impossible to pin down. In your case, Shirley, the single umbilical artery may have affected blood flow to the developing fetus. Also, although John did not have jaundice at birth, we know that there was an ABO blood incompatibility present during one of your other pregnancies, so that's another possibility. His low birth weight and your heart defect could have been contributing factors as well. It's just not clear."

"So, it's *my* fault?" Mom had always suspected her health was the root cause of several issues her babies had been born with. My older sister, Kathleen, was mentally retarded, and my brother Jim had been through multiple surgeries from birth due to a hare-lip and cleft palate. I had obvious problems. In addition to being suddenly overwhelmed with guilt, my mother was also nearly frozen in fear. She was four months pregnant.

"No, Shirley, it's not anyone's fault. Cerebral palsy of one type or another occurs in approximately two out of every one thousand pregnancies. Rarely are we able to determine the exact cause. One day perhaps research will enable us to do so and possibly prevent this from happening. Our goal right now is primarily to identify specifically how John is affected by his brain damage and what treatments we can offer."

"Does he have it bad?" asked my mom, tears in her eyes.

"Cerebral palsy is classified into types and severity. John's is a mixed case. His symptoms are classified as the flaccid ataxic type of CP with mild athetosis and there is some questionable right-sided accentuation."

"What the hell does all that mean?" boomed my father. "Is my boy going to grow up a cripple?"

"To answer your second question, no. He will face numerous challenges in his day-to-day existence, but with hard work and a lot of support, he should learn to lead a normal, productive life."

My dad was afraid. He had heard similar words when Kathy was diagnosed. His racing thoughts and fear of the unknown translated into a simmering rage directed not only at the medical professionals gathered in the dreary room, but also directly towards the disease itself. A monster named 'Cerebral Palsy' had just appeared in the room, and my dad was ready to fight. He stood up abruptly, hands on the table in front of him, practically defying the doctors to tell him something that made sense.

"Skip the damn medical mumbo-jumbo. Tell me straight what this thing is and what it's done to my boy."

"Children with mixed typology, such as John has, usually exhibit both the tight muscle tone of spastic CP, as well as the involuntary movements of athetoid CP. Although John does show signs of both spasticity and athetosis, his most obvious feature is ataxia. This generally affects a person's sense of balance and depth perception." The doctor paused, turned a page in the file, studied it and looked again at Mom and Dad.

Dad still had that glazed look of a man bombarded with too many unfamiliar medical words, and the doctor struggled to make this simpler for my parents to understand.

"My patients often have poor muscle tone and lack of coordination. They tend to walk unsteadily with a wide-based gait, where they place their feet far apart as a sort of counter-balance. Toe walking is not uncommon."

"Yes, I have noticed that is how Johnny walks now," said Mom, still clutching her tissue as she reached over to put a calming and cautionary hand on my father's arm, silently convincing him to sit back down and listen. Pragmatic as always, she heaved a big sigh, accepted what was, and sought solutions.

"Will he need braces to give him support?"

"That is something we may consider down the road, Mrs. Quinn."

One of the other staff participants finally added to the conversation.

"We have also determined the fact that your son's bone age is that of a three and a half year old, currently about one year behind schedule."

"What does that mean to us right now?" Dad quickly swiveled in his seat to face this person who was a new threat to his sanity.

"Nothing in the immediate future, Mr. Quinn, although it's something we will have to keep a close eye on. We want to make sure that John's hip, back and spine grow as straight as possible to minimize any potential problems he might have as he grows older."

"But no braces right now?"

"There are some other options we will discuss in-depth as soon as we have finished passing along the full report of our findings."

"Okay. What else?" Mom sighed, pulling a cranky boy bored with his coloring book onto her lap.

"As you know, we performed an EEG, which gave us a good picture of your son's brain activity. Well, we found an abnormality in his brain waves that we just cannot figure out," said another doctor, the consulting psychologist.

"What? Are you telling me, my boy is retarded just like my daughter?" barked my father.

"No, not at all. Indications are that your son is of normal intelligence overall." The psychologist glanced through his papers. "In fact, his math skills proved to be greater than most children his age and he appears to have a lot of creative ability. There is just a disturbance of functioning originating in the deeper levels of his brain into the posterior head regions that we cannot explain at this time. The medical term for his condition is called dysrhythmia."

"He had brain damage in the womb, and he has abnormal brain activity now, yet you say he is not retarded? Are you sure?" Mom said, blinking back more tears.

"That's correct, Shirley," answered the physician who seemed to be in charge of the meeting. "Mentally, John tests out to be very strong. His IQ is fine. I have another physical concern though, that I need to tell you about."

"You mean there's more?" Dad slowly ran his fingers through his hair as he struggled to keep his mind from snapping.

"Yes, it appears from our tests that the right side of your son's face is slightly weak and there are small signs of paresis of the right arm."

"Paresis? What the hell is that? You mean my boy is *paralyzed*?" Now my dad was shouting.

"Not exactly, Ed. It's an impairment of motion, yes, but slight. The body often compensates to some extent. For example, we did notice his left hand is dominant. Therapy will also improve function. With hard work and determination, traits that John already shows he has in spades, he should be able to overcome, or at least learn to adapt to, his limitations in time."

"Well, I'll tell you all one thing, my son is going to be treated just like everyone else, no different."

Dad was clearly thinking how hard a time Kathy was having in special education classes. His frustration and anger suddenly gave way to deep introspection. Everyone was quiet for a moment.

Dad seemed to come to some internal decision and quietly asked, "He's not listed as handicapped is he, Doc?"

"Well, cerebral palsy is indeed classified as a developmental disability. John's case would not rate as severe. He will not require the use of a wheelchair. He is not mentally deficient and can communicate well. I would say that his symptoms are more on the mild side, although he will require years of therapy and corrective surgeries at minimum."

"Okay. So in my eyes he is normal, with some areas that we have to work on."

"You can look at it that way, I suppose. We have some great therapists here at Children's Hospital that will do all they can to help John succeed in life."

My father stood, now with clear purpose and in firm control of his decision. He jabbed a pointed finger into the air inches in front of the chief physician's chest and ordered in his policeman's tone of voice, "I don't want to see the words "cerebral palsy" or "handicapped" listed *anywhere* in his medical record. If you doctors label him with that now, it will follow him around for the rest of his life. And I *won't have that.*"

Classic Dad. Although my father was not successful in getting the medical records altered, as a family we simply did not discuss the reasons why I struggled physically. My parents dealt with the symptoms and never discussed the root cause of my condition. Any question such as "What's wrong with Johnny?" was immediately squelched, and soon, no one brought up my limitations at all. We just did what was required and acted like wearing an eye patch or orthopedic shoes was as normal as brushing your teeth.

The Internet was not around when I was a kid in the 1970s. If it had been, I could have typed "cerebral palsy" into a search engine and come up with all sorts of useful information. I never pursued any informational avenue nor ever discussed my condition with family or friends. It was just something I had to deal with, adapt to, and keep under control. My parents downplayed the issue of cerebral palsy to ensure that I lived as normal a life as possible and I was never treated as someone with a handicap by my four brothers and three sisters. It was just the way I wanted it.

My grade school photo

3

Growing Up Different

I may have walked a little oddly but I was never sick. I had a fairly normal childhood except for one huge difference. A major portion of my formative years were spent doing physical therapy. Every Tuesday and Thursday, my mom would pick me up from school and drive me 14 miles to Children's Hospital.

Physical therapy in the early 1970s was not the same as today, there was no weight lifting, core training, or balance exercise routines. And if yoga, hydrotherapy, and Pilates were around, I didn't know of them and neither did my therapist. No, the gadget I used for my exercise was decidedly low-tech.

"Here, John, let me introduce you to your new therapy equipment," the therapist said.

She cut a length of heavy, thick, and dirty yellow rubber surgical tubing, tied it into a fifteen-inch diameter circle and slipped it over my legs just above the knees. I had to walk while stretching out this tubing as wide as possible. I looked like a drunken cowboy just off his horse.

The first time I tried this, I felt hellish pain shooting from the top of my head down to the bottom of my feet. My legs burned with fiery agony.

"Ahhh!"

My vision blurred as I staggered and fell.

My mom did not move an inch from where she was standing and made no attempt to help me up. Her silent challenge was clear—you can get your own butt off the floor, young man.

"You might feel some discomfort at first, John, but don't worry, you are just utilizing muscles that you've never used before," my therapist said with an unconvincing and forced smile on her lips that never reached her eyes. "The more you do this, the easier it will become."

Discomfort? Was this her idea of a joke? This was agony. I gave her my meanest look.

"Come on, John, let's try it again. Concentrate this time."

I slipped the tubing back around my legs and got slowly to my feet. The pain ran wild.

The next week she added another twist to the routine. I had to slip my forearms through the ring of tubing and, holding my arms out in front of me, stretch the thick rubber from shoulder to shoulder. This upper body exercise was to work my weak forearms and biceps, and expand my chest muscles. My arms quivered and shook after, as I strained to expand the hose.

"John, hold your arms out there!" my therapist would shout when she saw me drop my arms. "I want to get you strong so you can look pretty for the girls. Focus! You can do better than that."

At the end of each hour-long session, I did "competitions." I lay flat on my back with one leg up in the air. My hard-working therapist would try and push the leg down as I resisted and bantered.

"I am going to beat you today."

"Bring it on, big man."

Focusing with everything I had, I'd pretend my leg was a steel beam weighing ten tons. There was no way she was going to move it! On some days I was the Incredible Hulk, with thighs so strong and powerful that I could jump from rooftop to rooftop. Nobody beat the Incredible Hulk!

The therapist pushed my leg to the floor with no effort at all.

"See you next Tuesday," she'd say, smiling that smile.

After a few sessions I was introduced to a new exercise, one I came to dread the most and a technique that would eventually change the course of my life. It was called the "timed sit."

The physical therapist demonstrated it herself, sitting in a crouch like a baseball catcher, but with her back touching the wall and arms straight out. I watched as she looked directly ahead and used her arms for balance.

"This will strengthen your legs, John. Someday, you will be able to do this exercise without even touching the wall."

"I can do that. No problem."

The exercise *did* look pretty simple.

"Okay, then let me see what you got, tough guy."

She walked out in front of me, her timepiece at the ready.

"Let's go, John. I will click the stopwatch when I see that you're set and time how long you can stay in this position."

I looked over at Mom, who as usual was sitting in a chair off to my left, reading an outdated *Good Housekeeping* magazine and occasionally looking up. She just nodded and said, "Listen to the doctor, honey."

Determined to do this, I got down in the squat with my arms out in front of me, my back firmly against the wall. Burning pain immediately shot up from the back of my legs. My body started to spasm uncontrollably and I collapsed in a heap on the floor. I had lasted three seconds.

"Let's go again," said the Administer of Pain.

A few months later, I was buttoning my shirt after another rigorous session. I overheard Mom as she spoke with one of the hospital staff.

"That's a great idea, Shirley, you can take as much as you need."

Take as much as she needed of what? I wondered.

"And if you ever need more, just let me know and I'll get you some fresh material."

"Great. We do appreciate it," said Mom.

We do? Appreciate what?

"Come here, John, and help me carry this to the car."

Oh no. It can't be. Mom handed me six brand new pieces of surgical tubing.

"There is no reason on earth that we can't do some of these exercises at home," she said.

"Aw, Mom, I don't want to. I do plenty of work here at the hospital!"

"Quit your crying and carry it out to the car. You hear me?"

"Yes, Mother," I moaned.

It was like asking a condemned man to carry the ax for the executioner.

So then I was doing exercises at home every day *and* going to Children's Hospital for therapy twice weekly. I tried not to think about what *other* kids were doing.

"Don't forget your workout," was a phrase I heard from my parents a lot. My brothers and sisters heard, "Did you practice your piano, Susan?" or "Michael, is your homework done?" But for months on end, all I got was, "John, did you finish your exercises today?"

One day, as I arrived home from school, Mom was sitting in the kitchen gabbing with a neighbor, Mrs. Bennett. They abruptly hushed as I shuffled into the kitchen to grab a quick snack.

"Dinner's at five. Don't you eat too much."

"Okay, Mom. Hi, Mrs. Bennett."

"How're you doing, John? Have a great day in school?"

"It was okay," I mumbled as I bit into a crisp, yellow apple. I had gotten the last one in the fridge. With seven siblings, you had to move quickly to get food in my house.

"John, why don't you show Mrs. Bennett the exercises that you've been working on? I know that she would love to see you do them."

I froze in mid-chomp, my mouth full of apple, the juice running slowly down my chin.

"Huh?"

"Yeah, John, your mom's been telling me you're making really good progress!" the neighbor lady said with too much enthusiasm for my taste.

"Do I have to?" I felt a special agony.

"Be a good boy and go get your tubing."

This was in the 1970s; "no" was not a word you used with your folks.

I stomped up the stairs to my bedroom and grabbed the tubing I had hung on the old glass doorknob. My brother James was changing out of his school clothes, getting ready to play a game of Nerf football in the street with the kid down the block. He noticed the look on my face and asked what was wrong.

"Gotta go show Mrs. B. my stupid exercises," I grumbled.

"Have fun," chuckled Jim.

"Dork."

As I got downstairs, the show had moved into the living room.

"There's more room for you out here, Johnny. Go ahead, honey, take your time. Cathy, look at the tubing first."

The neighbor lady pinched the tubing between her fingers.

"Gosh, that's thick. You must be getting pretty strong to stretch this stuff."

Whatever. I just wanted to get this over with. I slipped the tubing over my skinny legs, stretched out in an exaggerated manner, and walked across the living room.

"That is wonderful! You are doing a great job! Look at your muscles!" she crooned.

I felt like a dancing bear in a circus.

Weekly therapy at the hospital continued until my early teens. My muscles did get stronger as I waded through the physical and emotional turmoil of adolescence. Although my painful sessions with the therapist helped me gain strength and stamina, they did nothing for my self-confidence and social skills. By the time I was 13, I had built an invincible emotional wall to shelter me from most of the taunts and teasing about my physical imperfections. Home was my fortress. However, I was still a boy growing up in a male-dominated household, and I desired all the things most boys did, such as football, hockey, and wrestling.

We lived in a Tudor-style, two-story house covered in white cedar siding, with brown trim and a sharply pitched roof. It was the oldest home on the block, all my parents could afford. Next to the house was a parcel of land that my parents also owned. Out the front door, take three steps to the left, and you were in what my family referred to as "The Lot."

In the summer and fall, The Lot served as the football field where my brothers and I played a game deservedly called "Kill the Guy with the Ball." It really should have been called "Kill John." Not that I had the ball often, but I was a slow, awkward runner and easy pickings for anyone to tackle. I just couldn't get my body to do what I wanted.

The miscommunication between brain and muscle was most apparent when I tried to do anything athletic, like catch a football pass. When Jimmy threw a long bomb, in my mind I would make a grand leap, snatching the pigskin mid-air and immediately running for the makeshift goal. The reality was quite different. By the time I got my arms up to make the grab, the ball was already over my head. The time it took for my brain to process a thought and my body to take action seemed to take *forever*. It's almost as if I was using a cumbersome dial-up modem while everyone else utilized lightning-fast broadband. I would get *so* frustrated because I had a quick mind, but was trapped in a body that was constantly slowing me down.

This eager but awkward athleticism typically resulted in a mess. I suffered various cuts, bruises, broken glasses, and had grass stains embedded in the knees of my pants after every session on the makeshift gridiron. Mom shook her head, grabbed the big box of Band-Aids, and dragged me off to the laundry room.

During the winter, as soon as it got cold enough, my dad would run a garden hose outside and start flooding this same patch of land to make a hockey rink. I can still picture Dad out there at midnight under a cold Michigan moon, Pall Mall cigarette dangling from his lip, as he stamped down the snow with his foot. People from all over the neighborhood would come by and play some outstanding hockey games. A large maple tree stood tall in the center of The Lot and it was like having an extra defenseman on your team that you had to skate around. My parents hung a floodlight from the tree and kids skated on the frozen lot all day and late into the night.

I could not skate. In the rare event that I was on the ice, it was always in boots. I could only shuffle my feet, while everyone else glided around effortlessly.

But I was a spunky kid, even with creepy shoes and a body that wouldn't cooperate. One day, I told Mom that I wanted to learn to ice skate.

"Sure, honey, go ahead. Let's see if we have a pair of skates that will fit you." With my large family, we always could find a size to fit in coats, gloves, pants, and even ice skates. I borrowed a pair from my second-oldest brother Steve.

"Here, John, let me show you how to lace 'em up," Steve offered. He tied them almost painfully tight. "This will give your ankles some support."

I watched him closely as he laced them to be sure that I could do it myself next time.

The hockey skates firmly in place, all I had to do now was get from the living room, out the door, down the steps, and onto the rink. Leaning heavily on my brother's shoulder, I slowly made my way off the porch stairs to the smooth sheet of ice.

"Don't let go of me!" I squeaked.

"I got ya. Quit being a baby."

When we finally made it to the edge of The Lot, my brothers Mike and Jim were shooting pucks at our sister Janet, who was valiantly playing goalie. They saw me trying to wobble my way toward them.

"All right! Johnny is on ice skates!" Jimmy yelled.

They all came over to help Steve get me on the ice. I stood there, breathing hard, legs trembling from the effort. My ankles were now twisted outward in an exaggerated fashion and my feet were turning numb from the tight laces.

"Okay, now just push off on your outside foot," Steve ordered.

The ice skating rink in The Lot

I pushed off and fell flat on my face.

Steve helped me up. "Not bad. This time, don't lean forward so much."

I tried again. I went down hard. I was getting frustrated and my legs were shot.

"I know what we can do," said Janet. "Let's pull John along behind us."

So they lined up in a row and Jim, at the back, told me to grab onto the bottom of his blue parka.

"You ready, John?" Steve asked.

"Yup, let's go!" I said with a big smile on my face. And off I went, pulled along carefully by a chain of brothers and sisters.

I don't remember having to wear leg braces during those formative years. But I *do* remember wearing "special shoes" as my mom delicately referred to them. Heavy, black, and ugly, the shoes were used as a tool when I was a child to train my developing body to stay in proper alignment. One shoe had a heel lift to even out the length of my legs. I had to wear them all the time, even during the summer when all the other kids in the neighborhood were wearing PF Flyers and Keds. I felt like Frankenstein banging around with these things. In my dreams, I wore normal tennis shoes and could run like the wind. I could pivot on ice-skates with the grace of Gordie Howe, wrestle with my brothers and not get the crap kicked out of me, and catch the game-winning pass as time expired in The Lot.

Mostly, I wanted so badly to just be a regular boy and not be "different."

Big Time Wrestling was a favorite show on local Detroit television back then. I remember seeing matches between guys named Bo Bo Brazil, the Sheik, and Haystack Calhoun—huge, powerful men who went at each other with everything they had. Folding chairs were thrown, eyes were gouged, and hammerlocks were tightly applied. That looked like fun!

Much to my mother's dismay, my brothers and I would try and duplicate the moves of our heroes on the living room carpet. She wasn't afraid we would hurt ourselves. She was more concerned about the furniture with five boys bouncing around yelling, "Here comes the death grip!" or "Watch out for my sleeper hold!"

Although she enlisted Dad to be the disciplinarian, he was no help. He even joined in the fun. I can remember many times after dinner, jumping on top of my father, putting him in a headlock and hanging on for dear life. Then one of my brothers would grab the back of Dad's Fruit of the Looms and pull up with all his strength, yelling, "Hinder binder!"

Dad would retaliate by lifting up our shirts and rubbing his five o'clock shadow into our exposed bellies until we begged and screamed for forgiveness.

One time, Jimmy, Joe, and I were wrestling with Dad when suddenly he put his hands quickly up to his face, howling in pain.

"Oh my nose!... I think I broke my nose!"

My younger brothers and I got very quiet. Dad rose up, his hands cupped over the front of his face as he rushed out of the room.

"You did it!" I told Jim.

"No, I didn't. It was you!"

I just knew that someone was going to be in big trouble.

I got up and bravely went into the kitchen to see how Dad was doing. There he was, standing in front of the refrigerator with a ketchup bottle in his hand, carefully pouring the contents into his handkerchief! What a faker. Busted!

When I got to the seventh grade, I learned that my junior high school had a wrestling team. I wanted in on some of that action!

Joining the school wrestling team had been what you might call a hare-brained idea for a kid with CP. The reasons why I did are as complex as young boys themselves. Besides, it looked like fun!

So one day at the dinner table I asked my parents if I could try out for the squad.

After a moment's hesitation, my dad said, "Sure, I don't see why not. But promise me one thing. You won't come home crying, saying it's too hard. If you join the team, don't quit. If you start something, you better finish it, mister."

I'd met Phil Freeman on the first day of wrestling practice. He was in eighth grade and I was in seventh. Phil was the same weight as me, although a lot shorter.

At that first practice he taught me the rigor of drills, the viciousness of takedowns, breakdowns and pins, and the extremely high work ethic that defined him as a wrestler and a person.

In short, he kicked my butt up one side of the mat and down the other.

He may have figured he could get rid of me after the first practice but I kept showing up, day after day. It was two weeks into practice before I could take him down. I think he was nearly out of gas at that point.

"That's two points," I said.

Later on in the locker room, as we sat together on the bench, the coach called me into his office. When I came out, trying valiantly to hide the tears, Phil asked, "What's up?"

"Coach told me to take a hike. He said I was wasting my time and everyone else's."

Phil stared at me for about three seconds, sprang to his feet, and marched into the coach's office.

After Phil left his office, I learned that I was to stay on the team. I did not know what they discussed at the time, but I discovered years later that Phil told the coach that if I went, he went.

Imagine an eighth grader putting it all on the line for a seventh grader, someone he had just met a couple of weeks earlier. Because of Phil, I wrestled all the way through junior high and high school. The coach had made me Phil's project.

The wrestling coach had wanted me off the team because I struggled from the very beginning. Even after three years of physical therapy with those damn rubber tubes, my body was still crooked and underdeveloped. I weighed 75 pounds in the seventh grade and was tall for my age. The coach did not know about my disability because I didn't tell him. Although he eventually realized I had physical limitations, we never openly discussed my condition. I simply desired to be part of a team and be one of the guys. I thought that wrestling would be fun, make me stronger, and show everyone, especially my dad, how tough I was.

What I didn't realize was that wrestling is a demanding, physical sport for a healthy person. Having a body ravaged by the effects of cerebral palsy, it took all my strength to keep from getting totally creamed on the mat. Not only was my lack of muscular strength an issue, but I had that slow dial-up for a brain. Wrestling is a lot like chess; to be successful you have to think three to four moves ahead of your opponent. With cerebral palsy, my brain reduced my body to a mere pawn, and a broken pawn at that.

Practices were held every weekday afternoon from three until five on the junior high gym/auditorium stage. The small stage was the only practice area the school allowed for the wrestling team. We rolled out the wrestling mats from behind thick, theatrical curtains, then someone would place wet, cold towels on the thermostat, causing the heat to spike. The stage often felt like an oven.

Then the pain would begin.

We started out with calisthenics. Coach would loosen us up with hundreds of jumping jacks, sit-ups, and squat-thrusts. My flat feet slapped the mat as I waited for the coach's whistle for the inevitable push-ups and when I went down into the push-up position, my body hit the ground as graceful as a sack of potatoes. I was always the last one to get back up.

Everyone also "ran the loop," a lap around the interior of the junior high building. The coach would time us, demanding that each lap be run faster than the lap prior. As I ran, guys would comment as they went by,

"You should sue those legs for non-support!"

"Do you have a fake leg or something?"

"What the hell is your problem, anyways?"

My teammates would sometimes stop and point at me as I ran my sprints or mockingly imitate my unique running motion, swinging their legs wildly and laughing as they came down the hallway. I never said a word; I was used to the taunts.

Ironically, most of those guys quit the team, not being tough enough to stay the course.

By the end of each grueling practice, I could barely stand up. My T-shirt would be soaked through with sweat, knees and elbows covered with abrasions from the wrestling mat. Those marks on my skin were referred to as "mat burns" and served as a wrestler's symbol of pride. I always seemed to have a lot of pride all over my body.

Odd as it might seem, I loved every single minute of it. I looked forward to going to practice, seeing the mats rolled out and mopped off with clean, clear water. I relished the heat of that gym stage, and hearing the sharp blast of the coach's whistle. I enjoyed running wind sprints down the school hallway. I didn't mind the mile walk home after practice every night through the cold Michigan winters.

Most of all, I liked being part of a team, not being treated differently and being one wrestler out of 35. It was fantastic. During the two hours that I was on the mat with my teammates, I was not the "kid who walked funny," or the "boy who was cross-eyed." During those two hours, I did not have cerebral palsy. I was a wrestler.

When I got home, Mom always had a plate of food warming in the oven for me. Sometimes I would eat. Other nights I would just go right to bed. No TV, no dinner, no books. I often fell asleep when my head hit the pillow, many times still in my clothes.

I know that my parents worried I was pushing myself too hard. One night, I heard them arguing about it down in the kitchen.

"Shirley, he said he wanted to do this."

"I know, Ed, but have you seen the burns on his elbows and knees? Johnny's entire body is black and blue, and the boy is so tired all the time now. He can barely make it up the stairs to his room at night. What happens when he really gets hurt?"

"If he gets hurt, he'll heal. Don't worry, honey, our son is a fighter. Let's see what happens."

I kept at it, hoping to get my shot into the starting lineup. When the coach came up to me one day during my high school freshman year and said, "Quinn, you are going to fill the 119-pound void in the local tournament this weekend," I jumped at the chance. Finally, after three years of blood, sweat, and tears, I was actually going to step out into the arena and wrestle against an opponent from another school.

"Quinn, 119 pounds, Garden City East, report to mat three," the loudspeaker blared.

"That's me! That's me! Which one is mat three?"

The excitement drove me to my feet and I started searching frantically for my headgear.

"It's on your head," Phil said laughing. "Come on, let's walk over there together."

My best friend had already won his first-round match, pinning a kid from our cross-town rival, Garden City West, in the first period with the same perfect fireman's carry he used on me every day in practice.

"Good luck, honey!" I heard Mom yell from her seat.

Dad was sitting next to her, gripping his program, looking like he needed a smoke. We made eye contact. He slowly nodded his head and I nodded back. It was time to go to work.

Phil and I made our way to mat three, met by the coach, who patted me on the back.

"As soon as the whistle blows, give it everything you have, John!" the coach yelled, as I was snapping my headgear.

"I always do, Coach."

I walked out to the center of the mat and was handed a green strap that I secured around my ankle with Velcro. My opponent, a wrestler from John Glenn High School, did the same with his red one. These colors would ensure proper scores were handed out throughout the contest. I shook my opponent's hand and placed my foot inside the circle. My heart was beating out of my chest. I heard Phil yell, "Let's go, John!" My whole world seemed to move in slow motion.

"Ready … wrestle."

And 55 seconds later it was over.

Before I even realized what had transpired, I was on my back, looking up at the bright lights of the gym, hearing the referee slam his hand down, which signified a pin. I got to my feet, watching as the ref raised my opponent's arm up, declaring him victorious.

Throughout the years, I became a much better wrestler, perfecting the moves that I was *sure* were going to lead me to victory. That victory never came. I lost *every single match* I entered. I believe my career record was something like 0-79.

I never got used to losing. I hated losing. Losing stinks. Every time I wrestled, I wondered if *this* would be it: the match where I would have *my* arm raised in victory.

I never got to know that feeling. Never got to step off the mat and have the coach say, "Congratulations, John, great job!" Never walked the halls of high school after winning the previous night and have someone yell, "Hey Quinn, that was an exciting match!" It would have been nice to be called a winner just one time.

And I did get depressed occasionally; ready to blame my lack of success on the fact that I had cerebral palsy. Sometimes I wanted so badly to let my coaches and teammates in on my secret, to stand up and scream at the top of my lungs,

"Don't you realize how hard this is for me?"

Well, no one was going to know the truth, no matter how I sometimes craved sympathy and a little understanding from the guys. I was raised to keep my mouth shut, work hard, and most of all, don't quit.

If I had quit, I would have missed out on so much. Like the time Phil gave me a nasty mat burn on my left elbow. I have reason to believe he did it on purpose, but I can't be certain. Anyway, it was a beauty—big, red, and bleeding. So what does he do? Say he's sorry? Offer to help me up and see if I'm okay? No, my best friend yells, "Green spray!" which alerted the entire team to pile on top of me and hold up my mat burn for closer inspection. During the fray, someone grabbed a large aerosol can of a green antiseptic spray from a nearby first aid kit and proceeded to empty the entire contents onto my ripped-up elbow. I had never laughed and cried at the same time before!

If I had quit, I would have missed out on the fun in the back of the team bus as we traveled to wrestling meets, talking guy stuff or listening to Phil tell very bad jokes. I wouldn't trade that experience for anything in the world.

But in the back of my mind, I used to wonder if 0-79 was a precursor of things to come for me? After all the blood, sweat, and effort, I didn't win one lousy match. If I couldn't even do that, how was I going to survive with cerebral palsy out there in the real world? Was I always going to fail, no matter how hard I tried?

Phil and me

One day, after my final wrestling season, Phil called me and said, "Hey, John, make sure you buy the *Garden City Observer* this Thursday. There is something in the sports section I want you to see."

I had completely forgotten that this was the time of the year when the all-area wrestling team was selected. The best of the best was to be chosen and it was a great honor. I opened the local sports page and saw the first and second-team wrestlers, many of whom I had competed against. Upon closer inspection, I noticed an honorable mention grouping, and under the listing for Garden City East High School, I saw one name: John Quinn.

I had made the all-area wrestling team.

I could not believe it. I called Phil right away. It had to be a mistake.

"Phil, what the hell did you do? Did you pay someone at the newspaper to put my name in there? If this is a joke, it's not funny!" I could almost hear Phil smiling over the phone.

"You know what I did, John? I was at the selection meeting, where nominations were being considered. I walked up to the empty white board and wrote down your name. That's it."

"What do you mean, that's it?" I wanted answers!

"As soon as I put your name up for consideration, the other coaches rose to their feet in unison and said, "We love that guy!"

Yes, the area wrestling coaches loved me, but all through high school, I never really found a place to fit in. Although I formed a solid friendship with Phil during this time, generally for me there were no fun-filled Friday night football games, prom dates, or fast cars. My yearbook is not filled with flowery notes or manly signatures and it brings back very few happy memories.

Although I had been a member of the wrestling squad, I didn't consider myself good enough to join the most popular group of guys, the Jocks. Those guys were looked at as winners, and as evidenced by my career wrestling record, I was no winner. I envied them because they were all powerful football players and tall basketball heroes. Jocks dated the prettiest girls in school and walked the halls with the utmost confidence. I didn't even have the courage to ask anyone to be my date at the senior prom, fearing not only rejection but also the nightmarish thought of dancing. The phrase "two left feet" could have been coined by someone who saw me dance.

In an ultimate act of desperation, I asked Mom to show me how to slow dance before attending a cousin's wedding one June.

"Sure, honey, I'd be glad to teach you what little I know." Upon taking my mother in my arms the first thing she said was, "You're slouching, John. Stand up straight and look me in the eye."

"Yes, Mother."

"That's good. Now, men always lead, so take your left foot and step over here."

I moved to the left, directly on her foot. Mom winced, but recovered quickly.

"Let me turn the potatoes down to simmer. It looks like we will need more time than I thought."

While the in-crowd drove cool-looking Grand Torinos, Chargers, and Mustangs, I was deathly afraid of cars. Their size, speed, and power intimidated me greatly and led to one of the most embarrassing events of my entire childhood. I failed Driver's Ed.

Being raised to believe that I was like anyone else, when it came time for me to get my learner's permit, my parents just signed the consent forms as they did for all their kids. Okay, it's Johnny's turn to learn how to drive. No big deal. At least it started out that way, but quickly turned into a major issue for me.

I had never been behind the wheel of a car before taking Driver's Ed. I didn't have any mechanical aptitude nor had I shown any interest while Dad wrenched on the family station wagon in the back yard. When I finally did start a car up for the first time with my high school science teacher in the passenger seat, the sensation was overwhelming. Adjust your mirror; right foot gently on the gas pedal; not too hard; check behind you. So much information to process—I felt overwhelmed before I put the car in drive!

It got worse once the car actually started moving. My eyes had a difficult time taking in the visual stimulation. Poor depth perception made other vehicles appear inches away from my door handle. Oncoming traffic seemed to fly by, the sense of speed actually making my body flinch. I became nervous, which caused my left foot to shake uncontrollably. It was readily apparent from the first day of class that I was not doing very well and it frustrated me to the point of tears. I remember my driving instructor looking over at me and asking, "What the heck is wrong with you?"

I just hung my head.

To make matters worse, there were two other classmates in the car with me as I struggled behind the wheel. They couldn't wait to get out of the car when I was finished for the day. Soon the entire Driver's Ed class knew what a terrible driver John Quinn was. The ridicule came hard and fast.

"Hey, Quinn, I hear that you ran a stop sign yesterday!"

"You're such a loser, John. Mary tells me you scare the hell out of her when you drive!"

"Better get used to riding your bike, Quinn, because that's all you'll ever have."

On the final day of class, my classmates were excited about graduating and getting issued learner's permits. Their excitement rubbed off and I was thinking that maybe, just maybe, I would pass also.

I mean *everyone* passes Driver's Ed, don't they? My hopes were quickly dashed when my instructor came into the classroom. Everyone fell silent.

"Can I see John Quinn outside the classroom for a moment?"

All eyes turned to me sitting quietly in the corner of the room. The snickers started before I could untangle my legs and leave my desk. By the time I reached the door, head hung low in failure, the chuckles had swelled into an entire classroom of laughter.

I rode home slowly on my bike.

Since I could not identify with the Jocks, and wasn't athletically or musically inclined, I wondered if I would ever find a place to fit in during my high school years. With a demanding Irish cop for a dad, I wasn't about to go down the path of a high school burnout either. I would have been bounced out of the house on my ear.

Besides, I truthfully wasn't comfortable with that group one bit. Everything about them was intimidating, from their appearance to their casual attitude towards both school work and the law.

The law was everything in the Quinn household. You had the good guys and the bad guys and bad guys did drugs. So, as much as I wanted to escape the reality of my lonely existence, drugs were just not an option for me.

Alcohol was something else. My parents' generation did not think for a moment that alcohol was a drug. Drinking was a daily event, completely woven into the fabric of their lives. When company stopped by, as soon as greetings were exchanged the same question was always asked "What can I get you to drink?"

And they didn't mean lemonade! In our house, as in most of suburbia at the time, the refrigerator always had a good supply of

Strohs in its dark brown bottles or Hamm's with its famous Beer Bear. In honor of the nation's bicentennial, Mom and Dad got patriotic and started drinking plenty of Red White and Blue.

It didn't matter if Mom was cooking dinner or Dad was in the back working on the Pontiac, a can of beer was never more than an arm's length from either one of them. For special occasions like holidays, Canadian Club whisky was in the top cupboard, next to the good china. Mom was Polish. Boilermakers and Highballs were as much a part of her ethnic upbringing as they were my Dad's.

I remember one St. Patrick's Day in particular. I was home watching the *Mike Douglas Show* while Mom was in the kitchen making the traditional Irish meal of corned beef and cabbage. I hated boiled cabbage but could tolerate corned beef as long as there was enough mustard on it. Dad had called Mom earlier in the afternoon, telling her he had to work late because some patrolmen had called in sick.

The *Mike Douglas Show* signed off and the local newscast came on reporting live from the Tipperary Pub in downtown Detroit. The St. Patrick's celebration was in full swing, with people holding up cold pints of Guinness Stout and green beer. I was wondering how they made beer turn green when a familiar face came on the television.

"Mom, Dad's on TV!" I yelled, shocked to see my father's face filling the small Zenith.

Mom ran into the living room.

"Oh no, I hope there's not another shooting or something. Your father called and told me he had to work late."

Dad was working alright. He was working on getting drunk, if that silly grin plastered on his face was any indication. Mom was not smiling.

"Well, that lying Irish bastard!"

Caught between these two teenage subcultures of Jocks and Burnouts, I devised a strategy to get through the challenging time: I would stay quietly in the background. Other than wrestling, I did nothing to stand out or draw attention to myself. I did not volunteer for any extracurricular activities such as the drama club, student newspaper, or marching band. Limping around East High with cerebral palsy gave me enough notoriety. My "stay in the shadows" strategy was even applied in the classroom, where I rarely pushed myself and was considered an average student.

Unless I had wrestling practice, after school I usually went up to my bedroom to bury myself in a novel. I especially enjoyed Michener, Tolkien, and Steinbeck. Burnouts had their dope to help them escape, I had my books. How I loved to read! It took me to far-away places. I would pick up a book and I was instantly transported from my middle-class existence to exotic destinations such as Paris, Rome, or Hong Kong; places I wanted to visit one day.

One of my favorite novels is *Papillion*, the incredible true story of a man wrongly imprisoned within the French penal system. The sheer determination he displayed trying to escape to freedom was so inspiring. With my body imprisoned and shackled by cerebral palsy, I longed to jump the wall with Papillion myself!

After graduating from high school in June of 1980, I briefly attended a local community college. My CP had not curtailed all of my ambition and I knew I had to do something with my life. But what?

I thought I would find my way in college. Computers were just coming on the scene and learning to program the new tools of the modern age would be easy. I could end up with a desk job—perfect for my situation. So I decided I would get an associate's degree in two years and then transfer over to the University of Michigan.

I had it figured out.

I figured wrong.

I was not prepared for college. Basic algebra in high school had been a struggle and I was not able to deal with complex programming problems put forth in RPG, Assembler, and FORTRAN classes. Those languages are now obsolete, but in the early 80s, they represented the future. It had sounded exciting. But while other students breezed along, I had great difficulty grasping even the most basic theories.

One particular day in early November 1980 is vividly etched in my memory. I was sitting in the family dining room staring at a computer flowchart and graph paper strewn over the floor. A textbook entitled *Basic FORTRAN Programming* lay open to the third chapter, unread. The large stacks of punch cards on the desk were Dead Sea Scrolls to my eyes. I was in over my head and, deep in my heart, I knew it. Burying my head in my hands, I heaved a huge mental sigh and admitted defeat.

College was not where I wanted to be, becoming a computer programmer was not my true calling. A career desire buried deep in my heart started to awaken and it had nothing to do with book learning, tests, and lectures.

I stared at Dad, who was sitting in the brown La-Z-Boy recliner the family had given him for his 50th birthday. He spent most of his free evenings in it, usually dressed in a T-shirt, red flannel shirt, and blue jeans. He was reading the latest Robert Ludlum novel.

Dad had recently retired after 25 years on the police force, and was now working as a security guard for a Detroit hospital. With eight kids, there was no such thing as retirement. There always was another bill to be paid and food to put on the table. At least he was down to just one job now, which I sincerely hoped would relieve some of the constant stress he seemed to live with. Not only did he provide full financial support for our large family, he was also the primary judge, jury, and disciplinarian. Perhaps it was his policeman training, but what he said was law. He made those laws crystal clear and infractions had consequences, often heavy-handed. Although Dad was a harsh, stern man in many ways, I respected him for his hard-work ethic, and his honest, straightforward approach to life. You always knew where you stood with my dad. There were no gray areas.

My eyes wandered past the piles of homework on the table and the paper on the floor, into the living room where a fire crackled in the red brick fireplace.

I knew what I wanted to do, what I had to do.

I gathered up all of the school material spread out on the dining room table: computer punch cards, graph paper, text books, and the expensive special pencils we used to draw our flowcharts. With my arms full, I walked over to the fireplace, moved the protective screen with my foot and threw everything in. The fire roared to life as I replaced the screen. I watched the flames leap higher and burn away my college existence.

"Um hum," Dad cleared his throat to get my attention.

I had gotten lost in the flames and momentarily forgot he was there. He looked at me puzzled while peering over his black reading glasses.

"Are we having a bad day?"

"No, it's actually a good day."

"Is that so?"

"I've decided that I do not want to go to college anymore."

"Really? I hadn't noticed."

I sat on the living room floor in front of the fireplace. The flames were strong and the warmth felt good. The decision felt good too.

"So, what are your plans now?"

I wanted so badly to share with him my secret ambition—one that I'd been toying with since 1973—but I couldn't bring myself to do it, yet.

"Look at me, John."

I turned my head and gazed into Dad's stern eyes.

"I will give you two weeks to figure it out," he said.

That night I was the major topic of conversation at the dinner table.

"Is John in trouble for burning his stuff?" Jimmy asked.

"Yeah, big trouble. He quit school!" Janet pronounced.

"Now cut it out, you kids. He'll move on to something else," Mom tried unsuccessfully to steer the conversation on to safer ground. Keep peace at all costs.

"So, John, what *are* you going to do now?" asked Kathy as she loaded her plate with pork and beans.

"Huh?" I mumbled through my bite of hot dog. "I don't know; something will come up."

"Something had better," Dad said.

That night the idea that had been deep in my mind, stirred and wouldn't let me sleep.

I tossed and turned and pounded my pillow while Jimmy snored contentedly in the top bunk. I was starting to recognize what I thought I really wanted for a career and argued with myself about the pros and cons.

I knew too, it would shock my parents. Finally, toward dawn, I resolved the argument in my head and fell asleep wondering how I would tell them.

When I went downstairs the next morning, my mom was already up, having her morning coffee while reading the newspaper.

"Hey, honey, you're up early."

"Didn't really sleep much, Mom."

"You okay, John? You look kind of pale."

"I am fine, Mom, just didn't sleep too well,"

I went off to take a shower and get ready. I had decided to join the Navy.

4

I Want to Be Like Him!

Why the Navy? Was I being compulsive or irrational? Why not just stay in town and get a job at Ford Motor Company or become a cop like my dad, grandfather, and two uncles had done? I'm sure Dad could've greased the skids and gotten me into the police academy if I'd asked him. I never really gave my military commitment any introspection before, but as I sit here writing this book today and think about "why the Navy?" a few memories come to mind that I now know lay the foundation for my deep desire.

In the fall of 1973, my oldest brother, Michael, came home from Navy boot camp looking mighty fine. He had attended boot down in Orlando, Florida, along with follow-up cryptology training in Pensacola. Being 11 at the time, his leaving for basic training was a non-event to me, but I do remember his coming home. Mom had prepared his favorite meal, lasagna, and all my brothers and sisters were very excited to see him again. He had signed up for the Navy shortly after graduation from high school in June of that year.

The entire family packed into the Pontiac Bonneville for the 30 minute ride to Detroit Metropolitan Airport. I can still picture that old station wagon: forest green with fake wood trim glued on the side, and three rows of vinyl bench seats. With eight kids, my family needed every inch of that space. The littlest kid had to sit on the partition between the rows of seats. Since seat belts were not in use then, my dad could easily reach back and smack anyone of us with one hand, while he drove.

I can still hear him saying, "Don't make me stop this car!"

Going to the airport was always a big deal for our family. Sometimes, we would go just to watch the airplanes take off and land—free entertainment for a budget-conscious family. That day was extra-special because my brother was coming home.

My parents were both heavy smokers and as the station wagon made its way through the Michigan traffic it became filled with tobacco vapor.

"Dad, can we open the window?" Suzie asked.

"Just an inch," he said. "I have the heat on."

After what seemed like an eternity, we finally arrived at the airport. I was glad to get out. My legs had become cramped and I needed to escape all that smoke.

Entering the terminal, Mom pulled Mike's flight information out of her large leather purse, and found his gate. Since this was well before September 11, 2001 and the heightened national security, we all lined up, noses pressed against the Plexiglas window, watching his plane taxi in from Pensacola.

"Wow! Look at the size of that plane!" exclaimed Kathy.

"I can see the pilot, Dad!" shouted Jim.

Joe, my youngest brother, didn't care about anything other than making foggy breath smiley faces on the glass.

As passengers started to deplane, we strained our necks to see who would be the first to spot our big brother.

Finally, a man walked off the airplane in a sailor's uniform. I thought I recognized him, but I was not sure. This man looked different from the brother I knew a few short months earlier. He walked with purpose, his eyes alert, and he seemed bigger somehow.

Mom recognized him immediately and Michael, seeing her, quickened his pace until they embraced. She held him out at arms' length. "Welcome home, son."

"It is good to be home, Mom, believe me."

"You look like you've lost some weight. Are you hungry?"

"You bet! Is the lasagna ready?" he asked, chuckling.

By this time, we had surrounded Mike in the airport lobby.

"Hey, Mike! Welcome home!" said Kathy.

"Cool uniform!" cried Jim.

I stood silently there with my eyes bugging out, taking in this metamorphosis. Dad and Mike looked each other in the eye and shook hands man to man.

"Good to see you, son."

At the baggage carousel, Michael pointed out his green sea bag as it circled around. I tried to grab it, struggling, until Mike reached down to help me.

"Man, this bag is heavy!" I grunted.

"Be careful. All my stuff's inside," ordered the Navy man. "Here, Big John, let me help you carry that."

After we got home, Mike took off his dazzlingly white sailor hat and threw it like a Frisbee onto the couch. The family filed in, eager to hear all the details about life in the Navy.

Mike removed his black pea coat and placed it neatly on the chair behind him—probably the first time he'd ever been neat. The thing he called a sea bag sat near the front door—itself a commanding presence. The questions and comments came like a flood, all of us trying to get his attention.

"Is it hot down in Florida?" I asked.

"Look at those shiny shoes!" cried James, reaching down to rub the leather. Even the edges of the soles had been painted a glossy black.

"Are you going to sleep in your old bed tonight, Mike?" inquired Steve.

"Let me touch your hair," said Janet.

We took turns rubbing Mike's short military haircut. I noticed that Mike's neck and arms were deeply sunburned. I thought he looked real handsome.

"All right," announced Dad, "That's enough. Give your brother some room to breathe. There will be plenty of time for questions. Michael will be here all week."

At the dinner table, I could barely take my eyes off Mike. He was just so *different*. He was in civilian clothes, but he still looked like a military man to me. He sat quietly in his chair, back perfectly straight, while there I was, slouching next to Dad with both my elbows on the table, tightly gripping my fork like a caveman.

As we were getting ready to start the meal, Mom said, "Well, it is just so nice to have Michael home. Did you want to start Grace tonight, son?" Our jaws dropped. Leading the blessing was normally Dad's job!

"Sure, Mom." Everyone now had their hands clasped for a prayer.

"In the name of the Father, Son, and Holy Spirit…" and we all followed in unison. "Amen."

After Grace, Mom cut the lasagna, asked Mike for his plate, and loaded him up with several good-sized pieces. Even Dad had to wait his turn, and he was *always* served first. Traditionally my place at the dinner table was at Dad's left, which meant I was passed the food immediately after he was. That night we both had to wait. The topper came later when Mom asked Mike if he wanted another piece of lasagna.

"Yes, ma'am."

I was in the middle of drinking a glass of milk when I heard this and the milk almost came out of my nose. Mike had just called Mom "ma'am"! Even Mom laughed.

"I am not a ma'am, I am your mother."

"Sorry, Mom, just habit I guess."

Later that night, my brothers and I helped Mike move his luggage up to his old room where Steve, Jim, and I now slept. There was a queen-size bed on one side of the small room and three bunk beds stacked on the other. Michael set his sea bag down and started to unpack his clothes. Jim clicked on the radio and tuned in the local station, CKLW. Jim Croce came on, telling us all about *Bad Bad Leroy Brown*.

"Kinda crowded in here now with you back," said Steve.

"Yeah, but it's not as crowded as it was in boot camp. You have 75 guys in one big room. And reveille is called at 0500 every morning," explained the Navy man, as he put his ultra-shiny black dress shoes in the bedroom closet.

What the heck is "rev-a-lee at oh five hundred"? I wondered. Sure sounded exotic.

"Don't worry. I'll only be here a week. I've got orders to report to Pensacola for technical school. The Navy is going to teach me Morse code. Thanks for the big bed, Steve."

My brother reached into his bulging sea bag. Everything had been folded neatly and Mike unpacked slowly and carefully. Another side of him we'd never seen. I noticed something around his neck that jingled as he stood up.

"What's on the chain, Mike?" I inquired, pointing.

"Want to take a look?" he asked, placing the chain in my hands. "They're my dog tags."

"Where can I get one of these?" I asked, green with envy.

Michael looked at me and smiled. "I'll tell you what, Johnny, when you get old enough, join the Navy and they will make a set of dog tags just for you."

There was another member of my family who wore a uniform, and that was my father Edgar, or Ed as he liked to be called. An Air Force veteran of the Korean War, Dad also spent part of his four-year enlistment at Edwards Air Force Base as an air traffic controller.

Getting my father to talk about his military career was difficult, but when he did, I was amazed to learn that he actually worked with General Chuck Yeager, the first pilot to fly faster than the speed of sound. I remember Dad tossing me the book, *The Right Stuff* by Thomas Wolfe, and saying in his off-handed way, "You want to read about my time in the Air Force? Read this." It was impressive stuff for an impressionable teenager.

Returning home after being honorably discharged, Dad joined the Detroit Police Force in 1955 to serve along side his father, Lloyd, and two older brothers, Bernard and Calvin. For a number of his years on the force, he was a member of the Motor Traffic Bureau. At night, dressed in a macho black leather outfit, he skillfully patrolled the highways of the city on his gleaming Harley Davidson motorcycle. I thought he was so cool. Dad

Dad in his motorcyle cop gear

worked the midnight shift, eleven o'clock at night to seven o'clock in the morning. Back then, policemen kept their vehicles at home while off duty. My brothers and I often stood on the street corner patiently waiting for Dad to rumble up the road. We had contests to see who would be the first to hear the large police cycle arriving.

Having not only a father, but a grandfather and two uncles who were policemen, greatly influenced my decision to join the military. Many of the same parallels were there: defending the weak, being part of something greater than yourself, and a sense of honor within your community.

One of the other things that impressed me about my father was his work ethic. He *always* seemed to be doing something. To support his growing family, Dad worked various side jobs for years. He sold suits at a men's clothing store, painted freeway underpasses, and for awhile, was a home delivery egg man. And when he wasn't working a job, he was busy around the house:

cleaning the garage, putting new brakes on the Bonneville, or watering the grass. Dad worked so hard that he actually made my brothers and me feel guilty watching the Michigan Wolverines while he raked the fall leaves. It's called *leading by example* and it was a lesson I would always remember.

Towards the end of spring, something remarkable happened.

My father was transformed each day from an intimidating, stern cop into someone who brought a smile to many faces, adults as well as children. People actually screamed his name when he drove by. My dad was an ice cream man. Fred the Ice Cream Man. The tough Detroit cop arrested bad guys at night and charmed little ones by day.

The ice cream truck gig was different than his other side jobs, and occupied far more of his day. During the ice cream sales season, which usually ran from late March until kids went back to school the first week of September, Dad would leave the house around 10:30 at night in order to report for duty at the police precinct by 11. Working the midnight shift, he would arrive home around 7:30 in the morning and try to sleep for a couple of hours. I say "try" because there were, after all, eight kids in the house.

After a brief rest, he'd get up, shower, and Mom would make him a breakfast of steak and scrambled eggs. Then it was off to Kelsey Hayes Ice Cream Wholesaler and Supplies to fill the ice cream truck. Located on Warren Road just east of Evergreen, it was the place where the truck was loaded up with all the good stuff that kids loved. With everything carefully arranged inside the white ice cream box, Fred the Ice Cream Man was off to the west side of Garden City to sell his wares until sunset.

After a typical eight hour day on the route he'd hurry home, have another short nap, take a quick shower, shave, wolf down another meat and potatoes meal, then put on the blue uniform with the black leather jacket and head out the door again. He did this for seven years.

From time to time I had the extreme honor of riding along with my father on his route. I was put in charge of collecting the garbage. People would come up to purchase an ice cream, see me

Dad with the ice cream truck, 1968

sitting there and ask the question, "Hey, Fred, who's the kid in the truck?"

My father's humorous response was always the same.

"That's just some kid I found on the side of the road. Give him that wrapper if you're done with it."

I wasn't like my dad, outgoing and friendly. My lack of confidence, which stemmed in no small part from my physical self-image, severely limited the degree of social interaction in which I was willing to engage. My fear came across as extreme shyness. I avoided people whenever possible.

Fred, on the other hand, could talk to anyone. He was adept at the art of conversation, easily getting to know which parents could afford to pay and who couldn't, which child had trouble in school today, and which teenager was expecting another baby brother. Looking his customers directly in the eye, Dad worked the crowd with a magnetic energy and social style that I envied. I prayed that I'd grow up to be as confident as my father.

"So that was two Toasted Almonds and one Strawberry Shortcake? That will be 450 dollars please. But for you... only 45 cents," he'd say with a grin.

"Hey, Pete, good to see you again," Fred called to the old guy sitting on his porch listening to the small transistor radio.

"Those Tigers are really on a roll, especially that Kaline."

"Millie, how's Doug doing after his surgery last week?"

Dad cared about these folks and it showed in his easy interactions. I took part in none of this ongoing banter. I just sat in the hot truck, wishing Fred would hurry up and get back behind the wheel as quickly as possible. I cherished the time I spent with my father alone. Because of cerebral palsy and the way I looked and struggled to move, I was afraid people would laugh at me if they saw me climbing awkwardly out of the cab. I would have died of embarrassment if I fell in front of Dad and his adoring public.

So I sat silently in the cab and collected the garbage.

In long pants, of course.

My dad was a role model in more ways than one. He taught me to value honor, hard work, duty, and commitment. When I think "why Navy?", many of my answers lie in my father's life lessons.

✧ ✧ ✧

In 1980, the U.S. Olympic hockey team made a run for the gold at Lake Placid, New York. I specifically remember the game against the Russians. The event was televised, tape-delayed, and replayed during prime time on ABC, with no ESPN or 24 hour news shows giving away the results beforehand.

In the Motor City, hockey is huge. Some fans even call Detroit "Hockeytown." People live and die with the fortunes of the Detroit Red Wings, one of the original six teams in the National Hockey League. My family is no exception. I attended my first hockey game at the age of ten at the Old Red Barn, Olympia Stadium, in 1972.

The Winter Olympics were always watched closely in the Quinn household. We followed the bobsledding, figure skating, and the downhill skiing events. But what we really wanted to see was the hockey.

That year, the U.S. team—a group of college kids gathered from around the country—were heavy underdogs heading into the tournament. Nobody gave them much of a chance to do anything special. In contrast, the Russians had been playing together for years and had become a nearly invincible, well-oiled machine. The Red Menace owned the ice, and it seemed their Olympic gold was all but ensured.

Russia also dominated political conversations. The Winter Olympics were being held at the peak of the Cold War between the United States and Russia. President Jimmy Carter had made the controversial decision to boycott the 1980 summer Olympics that were held in Moscow to protest the Soviet invasion of Afghanistan. People around the country feared that the Soviets would retaliate by withholding their athletes from the winter games. The Olympics were now a chess piece caught in the middle of a high stakes game between the world's two superpowers.

My family gathered together nightly for those two weeks, crowded around the 19-inch Zenith in our cramped living room. I was usually sprawled on the floor in front of the fireplace. Jim claimed ownership of the rocker and Steve pulled in some dining room chairs so that everyone could watch. Dad ruled each evening as king of the living room from the best seat on the couch.

A last-minute goal by the U.S. salvaged a tie with Sweden in the first matchup for our team. In their next contest, Team USA beat Czechoslovakia 7-3, and then Norway, Romania, and Germany in rapid succession. Everywhere we went during the next few days, it seemed people were talking hockey.

The two old neighbors who lived behind our house hollered over the fence, "Did you hear about the U.S. hockey team? They beat the Germans!"

"Four wins in a row is pretty darn awesome. Can they do it? Do you think they could actually win the gold medal?" the guys in the barbershop wondered.

"Impossible," some college kids at the bar said, echoing the worry of many others. "Not with the Russians out there."

The Russians. In the other bracket, they remained undefeated, destroying everyone in their path. The way the tournament was set up, the U.S. and Russia met in the very first game of the medal round.

The day before the big showdown dragged, with school, dinner, and homework seeming to last forever, I avoided the evening newscast for fear that I would somehow hear the score. When the game finally came on at eight o'clock that night, I was ready.

And I watched and watched, not moving from my spot. The U.S. got outplayed in the beginning, kept in the game by their goalie, Jim Craig. Down 2-1 in the final seconds of the first period, Mark Johnson put in a rebound with one second left.

My brothers and I went nuts. "It went in!" I cried. The U.S. team was now even with the best team in the world, 2-2.

In the second period, the tension mounted in both the arena and our living room as the Americans managed a meager two shots on goal, staying in the game because of the outstanding play of Jim Craig. He was brilliant, stopping wave after red wave of Russian attacks. He only gave up one goal and Team USA was down 3-2 after two periods.

The excitement of the battle was palpable, bleeding through the TV screen straight into my bones. I was exhausted. I could not believe what I was seeing or hearing. The crowd rose with one voice, seeming to will the players onward.

"USA! USA! USA!"

For the first time, I knew what it felt like to be truly proud of my country.

In the third period, the U.S. pulled even on a power play goal. We were tied! Could it be possible?

I tried not to get too wound up. There was plenty of time still left. Team USA was playing the game of their lives, but sooner or later the Soviets would quit messing around and crush this band of college kids. Suddenly, the impossible happened, taking us all by surprise. A clearing attempt was stopped, scooped up by the USA captain, Mark Eruzione. He skates in and shoots… HE SCORES!

U.S. was now up 4-3 with ten minutes remaining, almost half the period. I don't really remember much at that point other than the clock. It was moving in slow motion. It seemed like the game was NEVER going to end. Finally, Al Michaels, the ABC announcer, delivered what is arguably the most famous call in American sports:

"Eleven seconds. You got ten seconds, the countdown going on right now. Five seconds left in the game! Do you believe in miracles? Yessssss!"

Yes Al, if a group of college kids, playing hockey together for only 12 months, could come together to beat the team of the great Red Army, it's a miracle. If they could beat a Soviet team that had been playing together since they were children, it is definitely a miracle, and if the U.S. team could beat the greatest hockey goalie of our generation, it is a great miracle.

I watched as Jim Craig, wrapped in the American flag, searched the crowd for his father, and I got chills when Eruzione called the entire team up to the platform during the gold medal ceremonies. The chants shook the building,

"USA! USA! USA!"

Yes, I thought, miracles can happen.

As I sat there in my living room, I wondered what it would feel like to wear a uniform and represent my country, like my dad, brother, and the players in the U.S. hockey team.

The foundation for my decision was now poured and set. But could I overcome my own great odds? Face my fears and do the impossible?

It might take a miracle.

5

The Lying Begins

On the morning of the biggest decision of my young life, I sat on my bed for a long time, thinking that from then on, everything was going to change. I thought about calling Phil to tell him my plans, but put it off for fear he would try and talk me out of it. I decided to call him when he got home, after the deed was done. Phil was everything I was not. He became the senior class president. I was socially inept. Phil was a gifted athlete, graceful and smooth. I was awkward and clumsy. The fact that we were best friends had a lot of people scratching their heads. But we *were* best friends and I was honored.

Phil was also the one non-medical person outside my family who knew about my cerebral palsy.

Sitting on the edge of my bed, I looked around the bedroom of my youth; I noticed things in a new light. They seemed childish. On one end of the oaken four-drawer dresser that I shared with my brothers, my worn baseball glove laid next to a small metal, red, white, and blue mailbox bank. Hundreds of baseball cards that Jim and I had collected over the years were in an old shoebox at the other end.

It was time to let those things go. I got up and walked over to the full-length mirror hanging on the back of the door. I stared hard at my face, tried to look older, and practiced talking as manly as Dad. "Hello, my name is John Quinn." It sounded good. So I thought.

"Let's go," I said the words aloud three times, mustering my courage. It was time to serve my country.

I grabbed my coat, bounded down the stairs and headed out the front door. The cold November air whipped my face as I walked down the block. I felt a relief to be moving, finally taking action. It was a three-minute walk to the Armed Forces' recruiting office located next to a 7-Eleven convenience store.

My gut was in knots. I waited for traffic to clear, jogged awkwardly across the street, and cut across the 7-Eleven parking lot to the recruiting office.

Taking a deep breath, I entered quickly, afraid I would lose my nerve.

As I stood in the lobby, my mind spun. Large posters adorned the walls. "Fly Navy," Army life was "a good place to start," the Marine Corps were "looking for a few good men."

I had entered a new world.

My gaze was interrupted when a Marine sergeant poked his head out of an office down the hall and barked, "What branch?"

"Huh?" I replied, my mind still in a daze.

"What branch are you here to see?" the sergeant repeated, slower this time.

"Navy," I said in my toughest voice.

"Damn, I was hoping you were here to become a man. Pete, you got one at the front door!" the Marine grunted.

Within three seconds, a sailor was standing in front of me, pumping my hand vigorously. Tall and slender, with closely cropped blond hair, this man cut an impressive figure. He wore a black, long-sleeve shirt with black pants and matching tie. Rows of multi-colored ribbons were pinned neatly over his right breast pocket and his silver belt buckle flashed brightly in the early morning sun.

"Hi there. Are you ready to change your life today?" he said.

I felt a momentary surge of confidence as he seemed to ignore my nerdy glasses, awkward handshake, and oversized shoes.

"I just have a few questions."

"Sure, let's go on back to my office. We can chat there."

Before I knew it, he was the one asking all the questions.

"Have you graduated from high school yet?"

"How were your grades?"

"What's your date of birth?"

"You live here in Garden City?"

"Ever been arrested?"

He marked off blocks on a form containing a checklist. Things were moving awful fast.

"Have you taken the ASVAB test yet?"

I knew ASVAB stood for Armed Services Vocational Aptitude Battery, the results of which would determine not only my overall qualification for military service, but also for which specific jobs. The higher my ASVAB score, the wider my selection of eligible careers. I had taken the test my junior year in the high school auditorium. At the time, I thought it was a joke, something to keep me out of classes for a few hours. Now, it seemed my future depended on how well I did on that fateful day.

My recruiter seemed pleased that I'd taken this exam.

"That's great. Do you remember how you did?"

"I think I did pretty well."

"Wonderful, I can get the results here tomorrow. After looking at your ASVAB scores, we can determine what your eligibility is for jobs, or as we say in the Navy, *rates*. Do you have any idea which category you want to pick?" he said, handing me a catalog.

"Well," I thumbed through the thick publication. "I went to community college for data processing…"

"You have some college classes behind you? That's super."

"But I didn't like programming at all…"

"Don't worry, John. We'll find the perfect job for you. Just trust me." The petty officer, a naval ranking similar to that of a mid-level manager, smiled like a used car salesman.

After what seemed like a thousand more questions, he wound down. "I think I have all the information that I need right now. Wait, I do have one more question here," he commented without looking up.

"Do you have any medical conditions that I need to know about: asthma, heart condition, back problems, trick knee, anything like that?"

His pen was poised over the "no" block of the form.

I was ready for this question; I'd been practicing it all night. "No, nothing like that, except for my glasses, of course," I said smoothly.

He quickly checked the 'no' box.

The lying had begun. There was no turning back now.

I am amazed how I was able to pull off that lie. My glasses were coke bottles. In addition to having very poor vision, because of the cerebral palsy, I also suffered from "v" esotropia, a condition of improper eye movement.

The actions of the eye are controlled by muscles and since cerebral palsy involves a lack of coordination between brain and muscle, esotropia is common for people with CP. All through childhood my left eye in particular would wander as it tried to focus. I also felt my eyes switch from left to right, as if they were working independently of each other.

Sometimes I would be talking directly to someone and get a comment like "What are you looking at?" or "Pay attention… look at me, not over my shoulder."

And you would think my shoes would cause alarms to go off. Although the cloddy black shoes of my childhood had been replaced by slightly more acceptable versions, they were still ugly.

I also walked with a limp and my legs were crooked, mismatched, uneven and skinny, like bent pipe cleaners with feet. For years I had worn long pants, usually hand-me-downs from my brothers, even in the hot, humid Michigan summers, to hide my legs. Looking back at family vacation photos, I'm the one wearing jeans in the heat of summer on the Mall by the Washington Monument in D.C.

On that day in the recruiters' office though, the Navy petty officer just seemed happy I'd come. He seemed like a new friend.

Family trip to Washington, D.C.

"Why don't you look over that catalog of Navy rates tonight, discuss it with your parents, and I'll be in touch as soon as I get the ASVAB scores from your high school. And don't worry. If your scores are too low, we can always retake the test, okay? After that, I will schedule your induction physical, which might be in a week or two. I'll let you know, pal," my new friend said, flashing a bright smile as he pumped my hand.

I stepped out of the lobby into the fresh air, feeling great. All of the worry, doubts, and fear that I'd experienced earlier in the day were gone. I now had a plan, a future! I even had a new friend.

My mind flashed back to my brother coming home from boot camp—now it was my turn. Clutching the packet of information about the Navy, I marched home with a big grin on my face. I couldn't wait to tell my family.

When I arrived, Mom was dozing on the couch. The television was tuned to the soap opera *Search for Tomorrow*, and a pot of spaghetti sauce was simmering on the stove in the kitchen.

When my mother heard me come in, she opened one eye, looked up, then closed her eye again. "Hmmh…" she mumbled.

"Yeah, Mom, it's just me," I said on the way up to my room. Just as well she was napping. I needed some alone time anyway to sort through the big envelope that I'd been given.

I sat on my bed and looked at the jobs, or rates as the recruiter had called them, that were available in the Navy. New words leapt off the page. Boatswain's mate, electronic technician, Seabee. I read about what life was like on board a ship. I learned you don't just wake up in the Navy. There is reveille for that. And at bedtime, they sounded taps.

I must have fallen asleep because the next thing I knew, Jim, home from high school, came charging into the room. I jumped up, startled by the noise.

"Hey, John, were ya sleeping?" he asked. He threw a pile of schoolbooks up on his overhead bunk and then froze when he saw the brochures I had carefully spread out.

"Oh no, you didn't!"

"What? You mean these?" I hedged. "I went there this morning to get some information, that's all."

"Yeah, right, so when do you leave?" he asked suspiciously.

"Nothing has been decided yet."

"Let me see what you have there."

Jim looked over the Navy literature. "Well, that looks kinda cool. Have you told anyone yet?"

"No, I've been up here all afternoon. Nobody even knows that I went to enlist." The confidence I felt earlier in the day was slowly leaking out of me like air from a balloon.

"Everyone's going to freak! Mom and Dad are still trying to get over the fact that you're not going to college."

"Yeah, I know. Dad's really putting the pressure on me now that I'm past his damn two-week deadline. I guess this qualifies as "figuring something out.""

"Did you tell the recruiter about your legs?" asked James, point blank.

"Nope, and I don't intend to. They didn't ask me and I didn't tell them." I said, adding, "I should be okay."

Was I trying to convince my brother or myself? I also felt a healthy dose of Catholic guilt about the lying part.

Jim said that we would have an almost full house for dinner that night. Steve had joined the Navy and was currently sailing the Mediterranean, but Mike would be stopping by for a visit and some home-cooking. I hadn't seen Mike in a while. He was now living on his own, working for a local bread company. I wondered how he would take the news that I was planning to join the same branch of service as he and Steve.

"Good," I said. "I'll definitely want to talk to him."

Right then, Mom called from the bottom of the stairs, "John, Jim, come wash your hands and get ready for dinner!"

Get ready was right, I thought.

Jim and I both raced downstairs. My dad lounged in his recliner as usual, reading the *Detroit News*. The television was broadcasting Rita Bell's Four O'clock Movie: Steve McQueen in *The Great Escape* and I could smell garlic bread baking in the oven. Mom stirred noodles into a huge pot of boiling water. The calm picture of everyday life was about to get a big whack.

"Hi, Mom, smells good," I said, entering the kitchen, my appetite long gone.

I walked into the living room. Jim was already sprawled on the carpet, watching the movie.

"Hi, Dad. How's it going?" I asked, assessing my father's mood. I could see right away that he was still ticked at me for quitting college. This was not going to be easy.

My parents were pleased when I told them the news about joining the Navy. But two weeks later the story was different.

I had gone to the Military Enlistment Processing Station, MEPS, to fill out more paperwork and take my fitness assessment. Then, after failing the duck walk, flunking my induction physical, and being told to go home, I walked out of the examination room and scanned the busy lobby for my ride. I just wanted to get the hell out of there as fast as possible.

73

I finally spotted my recruiter sitting in a faded green molded plastic chair, looking over some paperwork. He had driven me to downtown Detroit for the tests.

He jumped to his feet with a scowl. "What the hell happened in there, Quinn?"

"What do you mean?"

"I mean why the hell didn't you pass the physical? What went wrong?" He was beside himself, almost pleading for any answer.

"Did you talk with the doctor?"

"Yeah, he said there was a problem with your feet or back or something. What the hell? Is there an issue with your legs that I need to know about? How can you fail the exam? Everyone passes this thing. It's easy! Everyone!"

I couldn't look him in the eye. My focus was on my feet. My damn feet. I felt like such a misfit again, much like I did on the playground in grade school. "I'm just tired, let's go home," I sputtered.

"Wait a minute. I gotta tell you that I have been a recruiter for almost two years now and you are the first person that I've ever had that has failed the enlistment physical. You let me down, Quinn, I hope you are happy."

I let *him* down? He had to get in line! I now had to face my dad. What was he going to say? And Mom? They were so proud that I was joining the Navy.

Jim and Joe would be disappointed as well. Steven had left home this past year so I had graduated from a twin bunk bed to the luxuriously huge queen-sized bed. My brothers were already deciding who would inherit it when I shipped out. The debate had been going on for almost two weeks since James broke the news about my enlistment.

And what the hell had I been thinking, anyway, trying to join the Navy with cerebral palsy?

The military only wanted strong, fit men to join their ranks. I didn't measure up. I was damaged goods. A freak.

My head was spinning as we stepped out into the cold Michigan afternoon. The sky was gray and ominous and snow flurries whirled, biting my face as I jammed my hands into the pockets of my blue and white high school varsity jacket. I should have worn a warmer coat. My day was certainly not going as planned.

"Get in the car, Quinn," the recruiter ordered as we approached the black government-issued Chrysler K-Car. "I have wasted the entire day with you and I have to get back to the office quick. Got a six o'clock appointment with another kid tonight from Dearborn. I bet that *he* can pass the physical."

I slunk lower against the blue vinyl bench seat. Before I had screwed up the physical, my name had been John.

The ride home was deadly quiet. The recruiter was very upset. This obviously would not make him look good in the eyes of his superiors. With my failure, he would come up short for his assigned quota of recruits.

He didn't say one word to me during the entire trip back. It was as if I ceased to exist.

I was silent. I needed to think. What was I going to tell my parents, my brothers and sisters? I had relived and relived this welcoming scene… a brass band would be playing on the lawn with a Channel 7 *Action News* crew reporting live while my family gathered proudly on the porch, welcoming the triumphant arrival of John W. Quinn, United States Navy sailor.

Instead, I was arriving at the front door covered in shame and disgrace.

The government sedan rolled to a stop in front of my house, its tires crunching on dirty patches of snow and ice. Night had fallen and with it the evening temperature. I saw lights on in several windows and curls of smoke coming out of the chimney. Dad's got a fire going in the fireplace, I absently thought.

"Well, Quinn, this is our last stop," said the recruiter. I opened the passenger side door, slipped out and slammed it shut. My former friend didn't even shake my hand. The car quickly did a U-turn and sped away into the cold November night.

I stood outside for a moment. "So much for my Navy career," I mumbled.

I squared my shoulders, took a deep, frosty breath, climbed the stairs to the porch and went in the front door. Dinner had just finished. Kathy was clearing the table while Mom rattled pots in the sink.

Dad was at the fireplace hearth, adding some logs to a roaring fire. He looked up at me, "I thought I heard a car pull up. So how'd everything go?"

I just stared at my father.

"Not too good, huh?" he asked, as he swept embers from the hearth and replaced the fireplace screen.

"I failed the physical, Dad. They told me to go home."

He looked at me and was silent. My mother had heard me arrive home, and rushed out of the kitchen, wiping her hands on a worn kitchen towel. "So how did you do, John?" she asked excitedly.

"I didn't make it, Mom. They made us do this duck walk exercise and I kept falling over, so they pulled me out of line and that was pretty much that."

I still couldn't believe it myself.

"I am so sorry, honey. I know how much this meant to you."

"Yup." Tears started to well up in my eyes. I wiped them away quickly, not wanting to cry in front of my parents.

"Are you hungry? We just finished with dinner. Tried to wait for you, but weren't sure how long you were going to be. I can fix up a plate pretty quick. The meatballs turned out really good." God bless my mother. There was never a crisis that some home cooking couldn't fix.

"Sure, Mom. That would be great." I was not hungry at all.

Dad sat down in his recliner and we both listened to the crackling fire for a moment, lost in thought. Finally he said, "So that's it with the Navy idea, huh?"

"I guess so, Dad, but I was so close." I was near tears again. I couldn't help it.

"This duck walk exercise was the last thing I had to do before I passed the physical. If I had just made it through that part, I would be in the military right now, no problem."

My father looked right at me. "Show me?" he asked.

"What?" I said wiping away more tears.

"Let me see this duck walk thing that they made you do."

So I rose out of the chair and, with my coat still on, got into a catcher's squat as best I could. Unable to hold the stance, I fell over.

"See?" I said while scrambling up from the living room floor. "It's pretty hard, even for someone with normal legs." I sat back down in the chair, defeated.

My father gazed at me and simply said, "Life is hard, John."

I stared at him.

"Question is, what are you going to do about it?"

A couple of hours later, I was lying on my bed staring at the ceiling when Mom called up, "Johnny, Phil is here!"

Good. I needed to talk to him.

I went downstairs and saw Phil sitting in the chair by the front door, leaning forward with both elbows planted on his knees. His chin rested in his hands as he talked with Dad. "Hey, John, your dad was just telling me about what happened with the Navy today. That's a tough deal."

"Yeah, I am pretty bummed." I wanted to talk to Phil alone.

"Wanna go downstairs and shoot some pool?"

"Sure. Nice to see you, Mr. Quinn," Phil said as we headed toward the basement.

Going through the small kitchen, we grabbed a couple of cans of Mountain Dew out of the refrigerator and quickly went downstairs. We ran into Mom, who was doing laundry. "I'll be finished here in a minute, boys," she called out. With our large family, Mom was a fixture in the basement.

"No problem, Mom, we're just going to play a game of pool," I said, as we made our way over to the faded pool table centered on an old black and white tiled floor. Cardboard boxes and plastic storage containers piled against the basement walls insulated the room.

Phil started racking up the billiards. I loved my mother, but I was secretly relieved when she walked up the stairs carrying a huge load of bath towels.

I stopped my half-hearted attempt at the six ball and blurted, "I just cannot believe it!" We plunked down on a weary brown sofa by the near wall.

"What the hell happened at the physical today? What went wrong?" Phil asked.

The words just spilled out... how the physical had actually gone very smoothly until the last portion of the exam. Phil listened intently. He was a good listener.

"So then this doctor tells everyone to get into a crouch..."

I got up off the sofa to demonstrate and fell over, just like every time before. "So they see me fall, pull me out of line and that's pretty much it. End of story."

"Damn. You were so close." He raised his eyebrows over the description of the duck walk, but didn't laugh. We both sat in silence, thinking.

After a minute or so, Phil finally asked, "Did they mention cerebral palsy at all to you?"

"No. They just said they couldn't use someone like me."

"So you did *not* fail the physical because you have cerebral palsy, right?"

"What do you mean?"

"You didn't flunk the examination specifically because of your condition; you failed because you couldn't do the damn duck walk thing. Am I right?"

Phil began pacing the floor of the basement.

"Yeah, that's right."

"And you said it yourself: They didn't pull you out of line until you fell. Maybe if you had passed that last exercise, they would have never known something was wrong and you would be in the Navy right now."

"I don't understand what you are trying to say, Phil. I failed the physical. They won't let me in. That's it."

"What if you went back?" asked Phil.

"Believe me, I've been thinking about that ever since those doctors told me to take a hike."

With Phil in 1983

I remembered how ticked I was while hearing that enlistment oath and how I vowed to come back. But here, now safe in my basement, reality and doubt were sinking in.

"Passing that physical is impossible for me, buddy."

"Is it really?" asked Phil. "I'll bet that if you practice this duck walk drill, you would get real good at it. Then you go back, take the physical again and this time pass easy. Heck, you already know how the exam is set up and you flew through everything up until the last part."

"Somebody would find out, Phil!"

"So what!" Phil shot back. "Give it a try. It beats sitting around here, working at the Marathon gas station. Besides, you've been talking about joining the Navy for as long as I have known you. You have to try again. It's what you really want to do."

"I can't do it," I said.

"Can't, or won't?"

I looked down at my feet. "I'm just not strong enough. It was a stupid idea to even think I could pass a military physical." I could feel Phil looking at me but I couldn't meet his gaze. I was ashamed of myself.

"So, you're quitting then?"

"Yeah, I guess so," I mumbled softly, my stare boring a hole into a chipped black tile on the basement floor.

"Funny," Phil said. "I never pegged you as a quitter."

Phil had called me a quitter. Those words cut deeply. I'd never been accused of quitting anything in my life, and *never* by Phil.

I was at a crossroad. On one hand, I could take the easier path—stay home, forget about my dream of joining the Navy, and get on with my life… somehow. On the other hand, to answer my father's question, I could "do something about it."

The day after failing my enlistment physical I was down in the basement, looking for the one tool that had assisted me in the past. My mom didn't throw anything away. It had to be down here.

I moved some cardboard boxes and blue plastic storage bins to one side and opened the lids on a few others, stacking them carefully against the basement wall. I had mixed emotions; anxiety and fear were churning in my gut. But Phil's words—and my dad's—kept ringing in my ears.

"So what are you going to do about it now, quitter?"

I moved three more cardboard boxes aside to reveal another blue container. I opened the lid to check the contents of this one and amazingly there it was, like an old friend you lost touch with and suddenly found. A smile actually came to my face.

I reached down into the plastic storage bin and pulled out my old yellow surgical tubing. I examined each length of hose to see if they were still pliable and saw that several had grown brittle and hard over time. Another piece of tubing was still tied in a circle from the last time I had used it. How long had that been, five, six years?

Seemingly without thought, I slipped my legs through the circle of rubber hose, and stretched my legs out wide. I was immediately reintroduced to my old friend, Mr. Pain, who shouted, "Hi there, kid, remember me?"

"Come on, Mr. Pain, let's go for a walk."

One year later...

Throwing the tubing down on the floor, I walked upstairs, ready for that damnable duck exercise. Today was the day I'd been focusing on since being pulled out of line and told to go home 12 long months ago. I would go back and enlist in the Navy. This time, I would be prepared... or would I?

I had been so close last time. If I'd been able to do the duck walk, I would be wearing a uniform today. That thought haunted me—kept me going. And what were my other job choices?

> Wanted: Skinny, lazy-eyed high school graduate who walks with a limp. Dropped out of community college. Failed at prior attempt to join the service. Currently living with his parents.

Not many jobs out there for someone with those credentials.

And so, reverting back to the exercises of my childhood, I worked out every day in the damp, musty basement with tubing stretched across my legs. I leaned my back up against the cold, gray cinder block wall, crouched down in a catcher's squat, putting my arms out in front. Counting the seconds off in my head, "One thousand one, one thousand two..."

At first I couldn't do five seconds. Tears came to my eyes, and a combination of pain and frustration washed over me. Instead of a 24-hour gym complete with music and personal trainer, I just had some brittle rubber tubing and my thoughts to motivate me.

If my time on the wrestling mat has taught me anything, it's perseverance. Never, never quit. When my legs quivered and gave out, I got up and tried again, and again, and again.

"Come on, John," I would yell at myself, "one more lap around the basement." When my back burned with pain from the timed sit exercise, I would remember the voices of men taking enlistment oaths and try again.

Slowly, ever so slowly, my body got stronger. First, I set a standard of being able to stay in the catcher's squat, without wall support, five seconds, then ten. Once I was able to stay in a crouch for 30 seconds without falling over, I proceeded to take baby steps around the basement. I had to get this right. It's been said that the longest journey begins with a single step and on some days, a single step was all I could take.

Occasionally, my mom would be in the basement washing clothes and watch me doing the duck walk. She would never say a word, never question why I was sitting in a crouch with my back against the wall. She would just smile at me as I continued to march around the broken tiles of that old cellar.

I did this for 365 days without taking one day off.

Although I never came right out and told Mom and Dad the reason I was working out all the time, they must have known, because they never pressed me further about my future plans or pushed me to get a job. My parents allowed me that year, and their silent support made all the difference as I worked to make my body stronger.

I called Phil, woke him up from a nap, and asked him to come right over. He was a little confused, since he had just been at our house for dinner a couple of days before, but within an hour he was there and we went downstairs.

"I have been working on something. Watch this, buddy."

Getting down in my crouch, I put my arms out, and did not fall, wobble, or even so much as flinch while Phil circled me.

"Wow, John, that's amazing! How long have you been working on this?"

"Only about a year."

Phil smiled and shook his head. "Let me get this straight. You try to enlist in the Navy and fail your physical because you have cerebral palsy, but you don't accept this outcome. So you come down here to this cold basement and bust your butt for a year, just to go back to see if you can pass the physical again? ... and you don't tell anyone?"

It's true. I hadn't openly discussed my plans with my family or Phil. Before I did, I needed to make sure that I could successfully complete the one exercise that had sealed my fate at the last physical. As my friend saw, I was now there.

"Hell, Phil, it was your idea. Remember?"

"Yeah. But I didn't think you'd actually go through with it. You were so majorly bummed when you failed last year, I was just trying to lift your spirits! How much longer before you go back and try again?"

"I am going to the enlistment station this afternoon."

"This afternoon? You're going to see the recruiter this afternoon?"

"Yup."

"Damn, John, you're good at keeping a secret. I sure hope you pass this time. You don't think the Navy knows about your prior attempt?"

Phil had just voiced a concern that I'd had for the past 12 months.

"This is stupid. They will never let you in the door," a little voice in the back of my mind had been telling me.

Here I am, working hard to try to make an impossible dream a reality, and it may be for nothing. What if my old recruiter is still in his office and recognizes me? Was my name on a nationwide database of guys who had flunked previous physicals? Had my social security number been tagged with a note saying, "Hey, don't let this guy in the Navy. Something's wrong with him."

If I actually made it past the recruiter, what about the doctors at the induction center? Are the physicians still there that sent me home a year ago? Would I be laughed at again? Who'd ever heard of someone with cerebral palsy becoming a sailor anyway? I admit I had my doubts about getting away with this.

I began to think that the chances of succeeding were a million to one. Impossible odds, some would say. A million to one! How about one in a million?

My official Boot Camp photo

6

Learning the Drill

"He's here, Mom. It's time for me to go," I said, as a white government car pulled up outside the house.

I rose from the couch where we had been sitting together and let go of her hand.

"Do you need any money, John?" she asked.

"Nope I'm fine. Just give me a hug." I embraced my mom for the last time as a civilian. In the future, I would be wearing Navy blue.

"Don't forget your toiletry kit. According to your brothers, it's the only item you can bring with you to Great Lakes."

Mom was right. I would be traveling light for this part of the trip, with the Navy providing everything I would need in life.

Everything.

I was headed to Navy boot camp. I *had* passed the entrance physical. Nobody said a word about my legs, not the new recruiter, not the military doctors, nobody.

And of course, I kept my mouth shut. The examination went as scripted from a year earlier, except this time, when it came time to do the duck walk, I was ready. If there had been a duck walking championship held that day, I would have been the winner. I was the best damn squatter in the building. And my thousand-watt smile could have lit up Tiger Stadium.

Mom and I walked out to the front porch and saw that an inch of snow had fallen during the night. I hope Jim remembers to shovel it off today, I thought, bending down to pick up the morning paper.

Not your job anymore, John.

I turned and handed the *Detroit Free Press* to Mom, looking her in the eye.

"Okay, see you in a few months. Love you."

"Be safe, son."

Stepping down carefully from the porch and into the white government sedan, I looked back at the house only to see that my mother had already closed the door on my childhood.

"You ready to go, Quinn?" asked my recruiter.

"More than you will ever know."

"All right, listen up. When I call your name, get on the bus number that I tell you. Got it?" a voice in a sound system boomed. I was once again at the busy MEPS building in Detroit and had been sitting there for the past couple of hours. Greyhound buses were lined up outside, motors running, ready for the journey to Recruit Training Command, Great Lakes, Illinois, located on the shores of Lake Michigan. A chaplain had already stopped by to offer me a King James Bible, which I respectfully declined. My stomach grumbled.

"Porter, bus number 15! Quinn, bus number 15!..." the voice again.

"That's me," I said to no one in particular.

I got up and walked outside, looking for bus 15. Finding it, I fell in line and a young sailor, probably no older than my 19 years, took the large manila envelope that I had been holding and checked the paperwork inside against the name on his clipboard.

As I got ready to board the Greyhound, a naval officer shook my hand, "Good luck, son."

"Thank you. I think I'm going to need it," I said, but a smile couldn't be stifled. I was finally on my way.

"EVERYBODY UP! ON YOUR FEET YOU MISERABLE, CIVILIAN-LOOKING PUKES! YOU HAVE TEN SECONDS TO LINE UP AT ATTENTION FOR PERSONNEL INSPECTION IN FRONT OF YOUR BUNKS! BUSY DAY TODAY, LADIES! READY. GO!"

I was jolted awake as a large, metal trash can was thrown down the center of our living quarters. Welcome to Navy boot camp.

We had arrived late at night and after filling out reams of paperwork were given an itchy, gray wool blanket, flat pillow, dingy white sheets, and then instructed to get some sleep in a large, open bay room that would be our home for the next eight weeks. I felt like I had slept for a mere three minutes. The clock on the wall said it was only four in the morning.

"…THREE, TWO, ONE, EVERYONE HALT, RIGHT WHERE YOU ARE!" hollered a sailor with a red rope around his left shoulder.

I was standing in front of my warm bed, in my underwear, shaking from fear, exhaustion, and muscle spasms.

"You, drop and give me 20 push-ups," said the sailor who was evidently our leader to a man who hadn't moved fast enough.

The guy got into the push-up position and started quickly cranking out the exercise.

"You drop. You drop," was heard throughout the barracks as the Navy man ran from person to person, yelling out the order.

"I cannot hear you, ladies! I want to hear you count, one SIR, two SIR! Got it? Begin!"

"I am your company commander. See this red rope? It symbolizes the fact that for the next eight weeks, I am your father, mother, priest, and the only friend you have in the entire world!" The voice echoed off the concrete walls.

"What I say is the law. Do as I say and you *might* become sailors. Some of you will not make it through *my* boot camp. There are 75 of you standing here today. On average, ten of you will be sent home, crying to your mommies within the first week here. Question is, who are those ten miserable pukes gonna be? It's my job to find you, and I am going to start right here!"

The company commander (CC) stopped directly in front of me. He was so close that I could smell his toothpaste. He looked me up one side and down another.

"What is your name, sweetheart?"

"Quinn."

"Quinn, what?"

"Quinn, sir?"

"I cannot hear you!" the petty officer screamed into my ear. Spit sprayed across my face.

"Quinn, sir!" I yelled as loud as I could.

"You cold, Quinn? You're shaking like a damn leaf."

"No, sir."

"No, sir, what?"

"No, sir, I am not cold!"

"You sick, Quinn? I hate guys who are always going to sickbay."

"No, sir, I am not sick," I shouted my reply, thinking what the hell is sickbay?

"Well, then, Peter Pan, you better stow that shaking before I knock it out of you, got me?"

"Yes, sir!"

"You are on my list, Quinn. I will be watching you close. I think you'll be the very first one I send packing. Now, drop and give me 20."

Oh God.

The next 16 hours were a blur.

The company of green recruits quickly formed outside on a large parking lot, or grinder. As soon as we stepped out of the barracks, it hit us.

The cold. Mind-numbing arctic air that made my eyes water, my nose hairs frost over, and instantly snatched away my breath. Having grown up in Michigan, I thought I was used to the cold, but this winter experience was on a whole new level. Right then, the wind howled, sending a chill to my bones.

"Listen up! We are only going to be out here for 60 seconds. The actual temperature this morning is minus-15 degrees. Factor in the wind chill and it drops to a minus-30. That wind you feel is called The Hawk, and that bird of prey is definitely flying today, ladies. Congratulations. You are attending recruit training during the coldest winter ever recorded here at Great Lakes. Now, let's get you all inside before you freeze your little tootsies off."

We were herded into the chow hall and told to grab a molded plastic tray and fork from the large stacks in front of us. I was hungry, and looked forward to some hot food.

As we were about to be served, the company commander informed us that we would not be allowed to sit down for breakfast.

"Too much to do today, ladies. Going to make sailors out of your sorry butts this morning! I want everyone to fill his tray, but eat standing up. As you eat, slowly move toward the exit in single file. This is called eating in pass and review. No stopping and definitely no food taken outside the galley. Understand?"

"Yes, sir!"

I placed my tray under heat lamps where it was rapidly filled with scrambled eggs, pancakes, something that looked like corned beef hash and what is that white stuff? Grits? I had never eaten grits before. I moved quickly around the perimeter of the large dining facility, jamming a dry pancake in my mouth as I shuffled toward the door. The grits would have to wait.

From the chow hall, the squad was quickly moved to the barbershop, where our hair was buzzed off down to the skin. There was no barbershop chatter about sports, politics, or women. It was 15 seconds a head. Some guys cried, seeing their long locks heaped in a pile at their feet. Everyone walked out rubbing their heads and pointing at the guy next to them in line. It was a very strange sensation to reach up and feel nothing but naked scalp.

From there, we all headed to the optometrist where corpsmen were standing by to give the guys who wore civilian eyeglasses an exam for government spectacles. Known as birth control glasses, or BCGs, these glasses were so named for their overall ugliness and total lack of appeal to the opposite sex. You could have any color BCG that you wanted providing it was black.

Clothing issue was next. I was visually measured from head to toe by a civilian who must have done it his entire life.

"Hat size: seven and a quarter. Chest: 36. Waist: 30. Inseam: 34," he yelled to a gray-haired lady perched behind a large table.

I was handed items in assembly-line fashion, rapidly filling a large cardboard box. White underwear, wool socks, black gloves, T-shirts, coats, heavy work boots called boondockers—a whole wardrobe for a new life.

"What size shoe do you take?"

I paused. Thanks to cerebral palsy, my left foot measures a 10, and the right one 12 1/2. No special orders here, I knew one size had to fit all. The socks looked bulky, so I answered, "13."

The marching boots weighed down the already bulging container as I hurried along.

Once the clothing issue was complete, the red-roped company commander met us in the next room.

"You all look beautiful in your new haircuts, ladies; now let's see if we can follow simple directions to get you dressed as sailors. Everyone find the package of white boxers that you have been issued..."

✧ ✧ ✧

"Pivot with your left foot, you stupid idiot! Guide along the sailor to your right! You know left from right, Quinn?"

"Yes, sir!" I shouted to the drill instructor who was marching beside me.

The squad had been out on the grinder for six long hours, learning to march in step. My hips and back were hurting even more than normal. It was so cold that my legs had become numb, but I thought I could still feel blisters forming on the back of both heels from the new black boondockers I was wearing. They were proving tough to break in and it was impossible to walk, or march, in relative comfort.

The cold, the boots and my cerebral palsy were piling up into a painful misery.

"Well, it looks to me like you're having trouble. I'll have to give you personal attention when we get back to the barracks."

Wonderful, a one on one with the CC, and it was only day three.

The transition from civilian to sailor was like being caught in a fast-moving current... you sank or swam. From the moment the reveille call jarred me awake before sunrise to the haunting sound of taps at night, the pace of training was relentless. We were taught the correct way to march, leading with the left foot. We learned the hard way that stenciling uniforms is an exact science. We frantically memorized the 12 general orders of a sentry. We were instructed on how to make bunks in precise fashion, with 45-degree folds in the corners. And we learned quickly who to salute.

I got dizzy trying to remember all the details that go into making a sailor, and retired to my bunk each night exhausted in my efforts to keep up with everything. The adjustment to military life those first 72 hours had been simply overwhelming. And I still had eight weeks to go.

Our transformation into sailors was overseen by a short, slight petty officer second class with a quick temper and a streak of meanness in his narrow face. One mistake brought his wrath down hard and I was a favorite target for his fury.

One day, having completed Marching 101, I entered the barracks with the other guys in the group. We were met by a stifling heat that caused my eyeglasses to fog immediately. We had gone from minus-20 degrees outside to plus-80 degrees inside and it was a shock to my system.

"Get those pea coats off and stand at attention in front of your bunks. I am going to show you how *not* to march... Quinn— front and center!"

Oh, no! What now? I obediently walked out and met the drill instructor in the center of the barracks while the whole company remained at attention.

"Seaman Recruit Quinn, attention! Right face! Forward... march!"

I was paraded around the barracks, the CC by my side.

"This, men, is how *not* to march. Jesus H. Christ! Look at this guy!"

The sailors laughed.

All that work down in my basement for this?

I had to let Phil know how my ambition of military service was going so far…

> *Hello, Dickhead, I mean Phil,*
>
> *That is the favorite word around here. If you screw up on something, that's what they say, "Quinn, you dickhead." They scream it at the top of their lungs, nose-to-nose with you.*
>
> *Life here sucks, Phil. 4:30 in the a.m. comes and you got fifteen minutes to get your socks on (two pairs), long johns, T-shirt, pants, sweater, work shirt, boondockers, pea coat, utility jacket, ski cap, watch cap, gloves, and a towel around your mouth. Plus, in those fifteen minutes, I have to make my bunk in inspection condition.*
>
> *It was twenty-five below zero yesterday with a wind chill of eighty-five degrees below zero! We had to march to chow. Marching in formation is hard, but everywhere you go, you have two inches of ice! Everyone falls and then the company commander calls you a dickhead. He makes you do push-ups on the spot, maybe thirty or so. That is not hard, but you figure you are in full gear and you're tired because you got up at 4:30 a.m. And I have only been here a week. Shit.*
>
> *Actually, we really just started camp today. This past week we got issued all our stuff, you form a company, get your shots (I got six this morning), stencil your clothes (they inspect those so they must be perfect), and stuff like that.*
>
> *Well, I wrote you, now you write me. Tell everyone I said hello.*
>
> *Your partner in crime,*
>
> *Seaman Recruit Quinn*

"I wonder how bad these blisters are getting," I thought with a growing concern while slowly taking off my boondockers later that night.

I had felt the pain intensify with every passing step and it was a relief to get my feet out of the military boots. Peeling back the Navy-issued green woolen socks, I had my answer. It was bad.

I had blisters the size of quarters on the heels of both feet. They had ripped open, exposing fresh, sensitive, bleeding skin. The area around the blisters was red hot and my ankles were beginning to swell.

My feet. My damn feet!

Gingerly replacing the socks, I jammed my swollen feet back down into my boots, tying them tightly. Carefully walking to the CC's office, I stood at attention outside his door, knocked three times, and sounded off as directed.

"Seaman Recruit Quinn requests permission to speak to the company commander." I remained at attention.

"Yeah, Quinn, what is it?" he said, looking up from his paperwork.

"Sir, I have some blisters on my feet and need to go to medical, sir."

He looked up sharply. "Let me get this straight, you have some itty-bitty blisters on your pretty little feet and it's making an owie for you? Now, you want to take valuable time out of my training schedule so that you can get some corpsman to kiss it and make it better? Do I have the facts here, Quinn?"

"Sir, the blisters are very painful and I think…"

"You think? You *think*? You're not paid to think, recruit. That's my job. I can't believe you are interrupting me to complain about a couple of damn blisters. And pain? You don't know the meaning of the word. Wash your feet good in the shower and you'll be fine. Now, drop and give me 20!"

Yeah I did know pain, and I knew my legs. This was trouble.

Four days after my meeting with the drill instructor, the company was marching near the hospital. "Anyone who's feeling sick, or has a medical issue that needs to get checked by the doc, step out and report to sick bay."

My feet were killing me, especially the right foot, which throbbed constantly in time to my heartbeat. As I started to step out of formation, the CC stopped me.

"Just where do you think you're going, Quinn?"

"I am going to get the blisters on my feet checked out at sick bay, sir. They really hurt something fierce, sir."

"You're not going anywhere but back in ranks, recruit."

"But, sir..."

"But, nothing. You heard me. Back in formation, you weak little girl."

The following morning, I looked down at my feet and was shocked at what I saw. Both my ankles had swollen to three times their normal size and were painfully tender and hot to the slightest touch. Most alarming were the red streaks running up both ankles to my knees. I knew this was serious.

I tried to get to my feet, but could barely stand. My bunkmate noticed me struggling.

"Come on, John, get the lead out."

"Smitty, check out my legs."

"Oh my God! I'll get the CC."

As I lay back in my bunk, a million thoughts ran quickly through my mind. Paramount even to my health was the worry that I was going to be sent home. All because of my legs. It figured.

The company commander strode over, exuding anger with every step.

"What in the hell is the matter with you, Quinn?"

He looked at my feet and the blood suddenly rushed out of his face. He froze, and I could see his mind racing.

"Quinn! I told you to get into medical last week!"

Yeah, right. You bastard!

"Damn! What the hell happened to you?"

Within an hour after arriving at sickbay, I had gone through the intake process and had X-rays taken. A first-class corpsman was examining my legs with a concerned look on his face. It just felt good to sit down and have my swollen feet out of those damn boondockers. I was burning up with fever and dizzy from the pain.

"Wait right here. I gotta go get my supervisor. He'll want to see this."

"I'm not going anywhere."

After a few minutes, a naval officer came over. He had gold oak leaf clusters on his collar, signifying his rank as a lieutenant commander. He took a close look at my ankles.

"This case is bad, recruit. Tell me exactly how your legs got to be in this condition."

I told the doctor how the blisters started... the whole story.

"So, you reported the sores to your company commander?"

"Yes, sir."

"And he told you to just 'clean them' in the shower?"

"Yes, sir."

"I also understand that you were ordered to walk to sick bay today in a blizzard, with a 40-pound sea bag strapped to your back?"

"Yes, sir."

"You weren't offered a ride to the hospital?"

"No, sir. I wasn't. My CC just wanted me out of the barracks as soon as possible. He had my bunkmate help me pack, made sure I could stand up under the weight of the sea bag, then instructed me to start walking."

"I see. My boss will be having a little chat with your drill instructor about the way you've been treated. I'm sure that there will be repercussions."

Whatever.

The doctor looked at me quietly for a few moments.

"Seaman Recruit Quinn, you are one tough, stubborn guy. Let me explain the situation to you. I would guess that your boondockers didn't fit you very well. There's a metal strip in the back of the boot that rubbed your skin raw, causing the large blisters. You were wearing green wool socks, and the dye from the wool seeped into the open sores. This has developed into a condition called acute cellulitis, a skin infection that's worked its way deep into your ankles. As you can see by these red streaks on your calves," he said, gliding his right forefinger over the inflammations, "the infection is spreading, and quickly… If we don't get it under control, you could lose your legs. Hurts, doesn't it?"

"Yes, sir."

The doctor smiled and shook his head in amazement.

"Also, I can see by the X-rays that your right ankle is broken—stress fracture, actually. Do you know how that happened?"

"No, sir. I don't." I was stunned by this new development.

"What I think occurred was that the infection in your ankles caused your gait, or stride, to change, putting more weight on your right foot, which, in turn, caused the fracture. It's incredible that you were able to stand the pain for as long as you have. Most sailors would be flat on their backs, howling in agony. Here you come, strolling into my facility, through a blizzard, with the worst case of cellulitis I've seen in my career. To top it off, you have a busted up ankle and are not even complaining. Your pain threshold is extraordinary."

"What is the next step for me, sir? Can I go back to my company?"

The physician chuckled at my question.

"I'm afraid that's impossible, recruit. You are going into the hospital, immediately. First, we have to get that infection under control. Then the swelling in your ankles has to come down so that we can put a cast on that broken foot of yours. You'll be laid up here for two weeks, minimum."

"So does this mean my graduation date from boot camp will be pushed back?

"I'm afraid so, son. Now, let's get you to the hospital."

"Seaman Recruit Quinn, please wake up and sign this."

"Huh? What?" Slowly coming out of a deep sleep, I checked my surroundings. Yup, I was still in the hospital where I had been for a week. My legs were suspended in a harness, which allowed the sores on my feet to drain properly. The blisters had been cut open, scrubbed and remained exposed, the fresh air gently drying them out. The red streaks in my calves were still visible, but slowly dissipating.

I was a mess.

Looking to my left, I saw someone standing by my bed. He was holding a clipboard and gesturing at me with a pen.

"Sign this, recruit."

"What is it, sir?" I asked, still clearing the cobwebs from my head.

"These are your discharge papers. Once you sign, and are healthy enough, we will send you home."

"Sir?" was all that I could voice at the moment. Tears came quickly to my eyes.

"Your legs have really taken a pounding the past couple of weeks and the staff here feels that discharging you is in your best interest."

"In my best interest, sir?"

"That's right. Just sign this paperwork and I'll have the personnel man come over to discuss the details of your discharge."

After all that effort to get here, my Navy career would end with a stroke of a cheap government pen? Just sign my name.

"I need a phone."

"What? Why do you need a phone? Who are you going to call?" The commander seemed to be taken off-guard by my request.

"I just need to make a call, sir."

"Okay, recruit, I can get a phone brought over here for you. Then I'll come back in 30 minutes for your signature."

I watched him talk with the duty corpsman and shortly after, an actual pay phone, just like those in a phone booth, was wheeled over to my bedside.

I could hear the operator. "Collect call from John. Will you accept the charges?"

"Yes."

"Hi, Dad. How's it going?"

"Good, son. How is the Navy treating you?"

"I'm in the hospital, Dad." My voice cracked.

"What happened, John?"

"I've developed some really bad blisters that got infected, and my right ankle is broken."

"Are you going to be all right?"

"Yeah. The docs say that I'll heal fine, but, Dad, they want to send me home. Something about 'it's in my best interest,' whatever that means. All I have to do is sign some paper that this officer is waving under my nose and I'll be home quick."

"Home? They want to send you home?"

"Yes, sir."

"Hmm." I could hear my dad thinking about this bit of news.

"Do you want to come home, John?"

"No, sir, I want to finish what I started."

"Good, because I don't want you back here. You understand me?"

"Yes, sir. I understand."

I realized the full meaning of my father's words as only a son can. Fathers always want better for their boys, and my dad knew there was no future for me at home in Michigan.

"I mean it, John. You belong to the Navy now, not here with your mom and me."

"I understand, Dad."

"Good boy. Now, did you sign the paperwork yet? Did you sign anything at all?"

"No, sir, I wanted to talk to you first."

"That's good. Don't sign anything. Tell whoever is there to kiss your ass. You aren't signing shit."

"Got it. Thanks, Dad. Say hello to Mom for me."

"Will do, son. Good luck."

A few minutes later, the commander, seeing that I was off the phone, came over to me. I noticed he still had his pen in hand.

"Well, recruit, ready to sign your discharge papers?"

"Kiss my ass, sir."

"Excuse me? What did you just say?"

"My dad says you can kiss my ass. I'm not signing your paper."

The naval officer looked at me for a full five seconds, turned on his heel, and left without saying a word. I never saw him again.

✧ ✧ ✧

"Is this Company 007? I'm supposed to report in here," I said to the sailor standing watch on the quarterdeck.

After spending two weeks in the hospital and getting a plaster cast placed on my right ankle, I was under orders to report to a new group, where my basic training would continue.

"Wow! Look at you. Are you all right?" inquired the watchstander.

I must have looked like hell with the front of my pea coat crusted with ice, government-issued eyeglasses all fogged up, and snot frozen to my nose. Walking nine blocks on crutches in the snow while struggling under the weight of a full sea bag had taken its toll, and I still hadn't caught my breath. This was not going to be easy. The doctors told me I'd better get used to using crutches. I was slated to wear this cast for the next seven weeks.

My new CC spotted me and came out of his office.

"You must be Seaman Recruit Quinn. I've been expecting you. Welcome. Come on in and have a seat. Seaman Recruit Richardson, take Quinn's sea bag and find him an open bunk, please."

Did he just say *please*? I gratefully slid the sea bag off my back and handed it to the watchstander.

"How's the foot?" asked the drill instructor as we walked into his windowless office. It smelled of black coffee and pine oil. I reluctantly took a seat on the couch, feeling awkward. I had never been inside my previous company commander's office, and I certainly never sat on his couch. Melting snow from my pea coat quickly made a large puddle on the spotless green tile floor.

"The foot is good, sir. Thanks for asking."

"That's great. Glad to hear it. I heard about what happened to you and I just want to say that I think it's a hell of a thing. It would not have ever happened in my company. I'm really glad you're okay."

"Thank you, sir."

Wow! Kind words in boot camp. It was nice to be talked to like a respected adult instead of being yelled at like a juvenile delinquent.

"All that being said, here are my expectations."

Oh no, here comes the shouting.

"You will put forth maximum effort in all aspects of your training. Bunk drills, physical fitness training, even marching. You will do everything the same as the rest of the company. Got me so far?" he asked in a quiet but firm tone.

"Yes, sir. I understand."

"Just because you're in a cast does not mean that you can relax and take it easy. That cast is not an excuse and I do not expect you to use it as one. Am I clear on this?"

"Yes, sir."

"Good. When the squad marches, you will march behind them, in the rear. Some people call that the sick, lame, and lazy platoon, but don't worry about this nickname. From what I've heard, you have been through hell and are plenty tough. Doc says you eat pain for breakfast."

"Thank you, sir. I will work hard in everything I do, sir."

"That's all I ask, Quinn. Now, go unpack and get your gear stowed. Bunk drill in 20 minutes. I am glad to have you on board."

So, under the calm and steady direction of a new company commander, I started to learn the intricacies of becoming a sailor. I stood my watches, made my bunk, and learned how to fold a raincoat. I participated in physical training (PT), was schooled in knot tying, and ironed my T-shirts until I could do it in my sleep. I missed out on nothing and participated in everything. And I did it all while wearing a cast.

It wasn't easy, especially marching around on crutches in the brutal cold, but I became more of a sailor with each passing day. I made mistakes and I paid the price. I did push-ups as punishment for improper deck log entries, for not being able to name the Secretary of the Navy, and because there were stray threads—Irish pennants we called them—hanging from my uniform. I was yelled at once for just being tall! I was treated like every other recruit, and that was just the way I wanted it.

However, my cast did give me a huge and very much-needed edge. I could now explain away my cerebral palsy symptoms. Whether it was my limping: "This cast is getting heavy;" my balance issues: "You should try doing a bunk drill with a cast on your leg"; or just standing at attention and trembling, the fact that I had a broken ankle gave me a built-in excuse when I was pressed to explain my physical shortcomings. Instead of being ridiculed, now I was "just the guy who busted his foot and got rolled into our company."

I was grateful for my lack of notoriety. I was Seaman Recruit Quinn, one of the guys. All my life I wanted so badly to fit in and feel "normal." Although boot camp was a physical horror, and I was still different due to my cast, I finally started to feel like an accepted part of something larger than myself.

"Hey, Quinn, the company commander wants to see you in his office ASAP!"

"What did I screw up?" was the first thing that came to my mind. You don't see the Red Roper to swap recipes and hang out. Something was up. I set down the iron I was using to put creases in a dungaree shirt and checked my appearance in a full-length mirror. Adjusting my gig line, I grabbed my crutches and hobbled forward.

"Seaman Recruit Quinn, reporting as ordered, sir."

"Quinn," said the CC, looking up from a stack of papers, "What the hell did you do?"

"Sir?" My mind started to race. What *had* I done?

"Get in here and have a seat for a minute. The cast comes off in a couple of weeks, huh?"

"Yes, sir. I'm really looking forward to it."

That was an understatement. After four weeks of trudging in cold, snow, and ice, my cast was looking and smelling pretty nasty.

"Quinn, I see that you came to boot camp without an "A" School. Is that right?" "A" School, short for apprenticeship training, is follow-on schooling where a sailor learns a rate.

"Yes, sir. I believe I signed up for something called the seafarer program."

"That's correct. You did. What a big mistake. Who talked you into doing that? Your recruiter?"

"Yes sir. He said it was a good deal."

"It was a good deal for your recruiter, but definitely not one for you. Do you even know what the seafarer program is all about?"

"Not really, sir." Things had moved pretty fast in the recruiter's office. That seemed like a lifetime ago.

"That's a program where you go to the fleet without a rate and get assigned to the deck department of a ship for a year. You with me so far, Quinn?"

"Yes, sir."

"Deck department is where you perform a lot of manual labor such as chipping paint, handling mooring lines, raising and lowering the anchor and many tough, demanding duties. Is this what you want to do with your career?"

"No sir. It's not." *Oh my God. With my cerebral palsy, I wouldn't last a week doing the type of physical work just described.*

"That seafarer program flat out sucks and your recruiter knows it. He sold you a lemon and you bought it. I'm just looking at your ASVAB scores. Hell, you're one of the smartest guys in the company and could have your pick of rates. How come you didn't choose a rating before you enlisted, Quinn?"

"I don't know, sir. I guess I made a mistake."

"Yes, you did. But we are going to correct it right here."

With that, the CC reached behind to his bookshelf, grabbed a *Catalog of Navy Rating Assignments*, and tossed it to me.

"Here's what I want you to do. This is important, so listen carefully. Go through that book right now, pick out five jobs that interest you, and write them down along with your social security number. You can do this right now in my office. Hand me the list when you're finished and I'll see what I can do. I'm friends with the personnel man, and he owes me a favor."

"Thank you very much, sir," I said, looking at the rating catalog.

"No problem. You are one tough kid, but I can tell you from personal experience that you don't want anything to do with deck department on board a ship. You will get dirty, wet, and greasy doing tough, topside work. It would wear you down to the nub. So choose wisely."

"Yes, sir. I will. Thanks again."

I turned back to the book. What the company commander said really opened my eyes to the reality of my situation. In a few short weeks, I would be graduating from boot camp and needed to think about the future. The thought of finishing recruit training brought a smile to my face, but the idea of being on my knees chipping paint from a Navy ship did not. With my condition, I couldn't handle that type of labor. What was I going to do?

As I worried the matter over, I looked around the CC's office. My gaze wandered past his chair and desk to the large stacks of paperwork he dealt with on a daily basis. Muster reports, personnel evaluations, and the plan of the day all demanding review or response. I had heard it said that the military runs on paperwork, I didn't realize the sheer amount of correspondence. I knew there were many sailors involved in generating and managing the paper flow. Even our company in boot camp had a recruit assigned to help the drill instructor with paperwork. Everyone in camp was jealous since it seemed like all he did was sit on his butt in the warm, dry office while the rest of us froze to death on the grinder.

Sit on his butt. Sit... on ... his ... butt! Then it hit me. Of course.

Get a desk job.

If I got a clerical rate, where I could perform my job primarily behind a desk, it would help hide my symptoms. Typing letters would certainly be physically less demanding on my body than chipping paint, and I was going to need every advantage I could to get through my four-year enlistment.

Opening the rating book, I eagerly looked for my future.

✧ ✧ ✧

"Hey, Quinn is out of his cast! Check him out!"

I came walking into the barracks in a great mood. My foot was indeed out of a cast, the crutches were history, and I was going to graduate in five days. Life was good. I noticed everyone getting into his workout clothes and I suddenly remembered it was PFT (physical fitness testing) day. I'd been so focused on getting my cast off earlier in the day that I had forgotten about it. There was no way that I could participate. I'd just had my leg encased in plaster for two months.

The company commander had other ideas. "How's the leg, Quinn?"

"Feeling pretty good, sir."

"Good enough to run 2.4 miles?"

I froze for a moment. This was the last big hurdle to clear before graduation. If I didn't pass, there was a real possibility I wouldn't graduate with my company.

"Yes, sir. I can do anything I put my mind to."

"Good. Get your gear on."

We marched the few blocks to the drill hall for the PFT. The team leader stopped me just inside the entrance. "Quinn, are you sure that you're going to be okay? I saw that you were limping a bit on the way over here."

It hadn't taken long for him to notice.

"No sir. I feel great." I was scared to death.

"Tell you what I want," said the drill instructor. "Run down the straightaway of the track just to see how your ankle holds up."

Because of my uneven hips, muscle paresis, bowed legs and flat feet, I have a unique running style that was about to be introduced to the entire company. The kids in grade school teased me to no end about how my body reminded them of a character in the *Wizard of Oz*— a cross between the tin man and the scarecrow. It was attention that I didn't need. I just wanted to complete the test and graduate from boot camp.

I sat down quickly, retied my government-issued running shoes, and offered up a prayer: "God, please don't let anyone find out I have cerebral palsy because of this run."

"Come on, Quinn. We don't have all day."

"Yes, sir.

Focusing hard on not running like the tin man, I jogged down the track, turned around and ran back. I could hear some of my fellow platoon members laughing as I slowed to a finish. The company commander quickly put a stop to the snickering.

"Company! Attention!" Everyone snapped tall, and any hint of laughter was instantly silenced. The drill instructor looked pissed.

"Quinn has just had a cast removed from his foot this very morning. A cast, I might remind you, which he wore through the coldest winter in the recorded history of this base. He braved exposed toes, a rotting cast that caused him to slip on black ice, and he marched in crutches. This guy has done everything we've asked him to do and more, and done it without complaint, in fact, with a smile on his face. He has shown more guts, determination, and courage than any recruit I have seen in my time of handling recruits. And this company has the gall to *laugh* at him? You should be ashamed of yourselves! Try running within hours of having a cast removed from your leg and see how it feels. Quinn is pushing himself to do this because he wants to graduate with this company! And how do you repay that loyalty? By laughing at him? Let me tell you something. I would sail with Seaman Recruit Quinn any day of the week!

"Now! ... Line up for the PFT."

The Star Spangled Banner sounded different in Navy blues. On graduation day, I felt a special pride. I could not believe the day had finally come. After eight grueling weeks of recruit training and a 14-day visit to the hospital, I was about to graduate from Navy boot camp. It was March 1982. I felt detached, as if the ceremony was for someone else.

My fellow recruits and I had been so focused on getting to graduation that the actual moment itself did not seem real. I kept waiting for the CC to say, "Listen up. After your graduation, we're going back to the barracks and do another bunk drill because I didn't like the way it was run this morning."

There would be no more bunk drills and no more marching in the cold or shoveling snow until the arms ached.

Hell, what do we do with our lives now?

We had gotten the answer to that question the previous night when the CC gave each of us our transfer orders to apprenticeship training where we were to be taught our Navy jobs. As he sat handing out the assignments, the drill instructor sarcastically commented on the rate each of his recruits had chosen for their military careers.

"Garner, you're going to be a radioman. 'Crise, Garner, couldn't you pick an easier job than that?"

"Luden, I see you're slated to become a boatswain's mate. Hope you like to paint."

Then, it was my turn.

"Quinn, I see that you're headed out to be a yeoman. Say hello to the captain of your ship for me."

Yeoman? Had I actually picked that?

A large yellow manila envelope was passed back to me and I quickly pulled out a set of my transfer orders to get a closer look. The document stated that I was to proceed immediately upon graduation to Naval Training Center, Meridian, Mississippi.

What the hell does a yeoman do anyway? I couldn't remember. It had been so long since I handed in my list of five possible jobs. And where the hell is Mississippi?

I saw that the book I had used to make my choice was being passed around the company. I wasn't the only sailor who couldn't remember his job selection. Finally, the *Catalog of Navy Ratings* came my way and I quickly looked up what a yeoman does:

Yeoman (YN): Duties include preparing, typing and routing correspondence and reports, organizing and maintaining files, receiving office visitors and handling telephone conversations, operating electric and manual typewriters, performing officer personnel administration, maintaining service records and official publications, performing administrative functions for legal proceedings, and serving as office managers.

I had gotten my desk job. I'd be sitting down at a typewriter and not standing on the deck of a rolling ship helping raise the anchor.

As I stood at attention during the graduation review, I scanned the crowd for my parents. Mom and Dad had written to me saying that they were going to be there for the ceremony. The stands were full and I was unable to make them out. But I knew I would see them soon. Besides, I had other things on my mind.

Like not passing out.

Eight companies were graduating that day and the advice to each recruit was simple: when you stand at attention, don't lock your knees; if you do, it won't take long until your legs give out and you collapse.

When we were told this, everyone chuckled. "No way am I going to pass out!" was the common sentiment throughout the company. "First one to drop is a wimp!"

After eight grueling weeks of boot camp, everyone got a good laugh at the thought of fainting during a simple graduation ceremony.

Just an hour into the proceedings, the first recruit fell. Boom! Right to the floor! It scared the crap out of me when I heard it. From my vantage point in the back ranks, I saw that several other sailors were wobbling, getting ready to drop. The officials were expecting it and had positioned medical personnel throughout the drill hall to assist those who went down.

No one was laughing now.

How did I do, standing at attention for over two hours? The sailor with cerebral palsy who had blood poisoning drained from both legs and a cast recently removed did not faint. He stood like a rock. A smiling rock.

"There he is! Ed, over there!" I heard my mom's voice above the din as I slowly made my way through the large crowd.

Boot camp was over. I was a proud United States Navy sailor.

"Hi, Mom."

"John, is that really you?" asked my mother, who held me at arms length in feigned disbelief. Mom's special occasion pink polyester dress flapped in the breeze, but her hair was held stiffly in place with Aqua Net hairspray. She looked beautiful.

"Hi, Dad. Thanks for coming," I said, shaking hands.

My father was wearing the only sports coat that he owned, a green plaid number he had worn for at least ten years.

"Would not have missed it for the world, John," he said, a proud smile lighting up his face.

I had seen that grin before, in 1973 when my brother Mike came home wearing his Navy uniform. I know my parents always regretted not being able to attend Mike's boot camp graduation. With so many kids, vacation time was often spent close to home.

"Are you ready to get out of here?" he asked. "Thanks to our income-tax refund, we were able to get a room at the Hilton in downtown Chicago. Your company graduation party is being held there, let's go get a steak and celebrate!"

I felt honored. I knew my folks normally didn't have the resources to pay for rooms at a swanky place like the Hilton.

Later on that night there was a huge party for all graduating sailors in the hotel lobby. I introduced my parents to the man who had been my military dad for the past eight weeks.

"Thanks for taking care of John, sir," said my mom.

"The pleasure was all mine, Mrs. Quinn. Your boy is one tough SOB; let me tell you. He's got a lot of fight in him."

"That he does," said my father, patting me on the back.

"Take care of yourself, John, and best of luck in your naval career."

"Thanks for all your support and patience with me, sir," I said, thinking back at how helpful he'd been. We shook hands and he walked away.

"Nice man," said Mom.

"Yes, he is. I was very fortunate to get rolled back to a company under his care."

"He sure thinks highly of you, son," said Dad. "Heck, this occasion calls for a beer." Flagging down a waiter, Dad asked me what I was drinking.

Huh? What I was drinking? That was a question Dad had never asked me before. "B-B-B-Budweiser," I stammered.

"Three Buds, please," my father told the waiter, who looked at me and said, "Can I please see some identification?"

"What? Oh, yeah. Sure," I said pulling out my wallet and handing over my brand new military identification. Flipping it over, the waiter said, "I am sorry, but I cannot serve you alcohol. You're underage."

"Okay. Not a problem," I said.

"Yeah, it's a problem. Bring my son his beer," ordered my father.

"I cannot do that. The drinking age in this state is 21 and your boy is only 18."

"First of all, he is not a boy. He is a man. Get that straight. Second, he's from Michigan, where legal drinking age is 18. Last, but not least, he is now a United States sailor who wants a beer. Get it for him right now."

I had never seen my father this worked up in public before.

The waiter was adamant. "You are asking me to break the law, and I can't do that, sir."

"You're telling me that my son is old enough to die for his country but not old enough to have a beer with his father?" The waiter said nothing.

With that, Dad stood up, "Come on, let's get the hell out of here and go up to our room."

As soon as we arrived, Dad was on the phone, ordering room service.

"I would like to have a 12 pack of Budweiser brought up to Room 703, please."

Within minutes, there was a knock on the door and 12 cold beers arrived. Thrusting one into my hand, both Mom and Dad raised their bottles and said, "Here's to you, son. Congratulations."

Best damn beer I ever had.

With Mom and Dad after Boot Camp graduation

7

Career Challenges

"You must be the new guy," a petty officer said while I was unpacking my sea bag. Sailors were storming into the suddenly crowded berthing compartment, rapidly taking off their uniforms and changing into civilian clothes.

"Yeah, that's me. I'm Seaman Apprentice Quinn." Introductions were quickly made all around. These veteran sailors were all part of my new team, the administrative department, and I worried that I would not remember all their names. They seemed in a big hurry and didn't waste too much time on the formalities.

"You coming with us, Quinn?" he asked, while pulling a blue polo shirt over his head.

"Where you guys going?"

"Anywhere but here," someone said, laughing. "Didn't you just hear the announcement for liberty call?"

"So, are you coming with us or not, Quinn?"

"No thanks. I'm pretty tired and need to stow my gear. I think I'll just hang out here." My training to become a yeoman in Mississippi had ended and I had received orders to report to the *USS Point Defiance,* a warship designed to support amphibious operations. The ship was on its first leg of a six-month western Pacific deployment, and my travel from Detroit to rendezvous with the ship had taken me halfway around the world to Yokosuka, Japan. I was jetlagged and wanted some sleep.

"No, Quinn, you *are* coming with us. Get your civilian clothes on ASAP and bring some money. You're going to buy the first round. We're in Japan, for crying out loud! You can sleep at sea."

In what seemed like moments, I was sitting at the enlisted club with my new shipmates, who were giving me the scoop on what life was like on board the *Point D*.

"I hope you like salt water showers, kid," from one guy.

"And powdered eggs with warm bug juice," from another, who was laughing.

As the night progressed, I noticed the time and stood up to leave. I knew that tomorrow was going to be a busy day and I wanted to look sharp when I met the division chief in the morning.

"Where are you going?" asked a third class personnel man, who was busy buying another round of beers as I was getting up from the bottle-strewn table.

"I'm going to get back to the ship and hit the rack. I'm still tired from my long flight out here."

"You just sit back down there, New Guy. We'll make sure you get back to the ship nice and early. Here, have another brewski."

What the hell. Well, another beer can't hurt.

The rest was a blur, then the fog in my brain started to lift. I was slumped in a rickshaw, one in a virtual caravan of Japanese carts pulled by runners. I looked up through bleary eyes.

Point D loomed above us, already awake and alive with activity. Glancing at my watch, I saw it was seven thirty in the morning. The rickshaw caravan slowed, finally coming to rest in front of the aft entrance to the ship.

"Okay, John, here's what I want you to do," a first-class corpsman called over from one of the other rickshaws, his words still thickly slurred.

"You see that small guy standing on the fantail with his hands on his hips? That's the chief. Get out and introduce yourself."

Following instructions, I, unsteadily and with little grace, hopped out of the rickshaw and looked up at the chief.

"Hiya, Chief! I'm Seaman Apprentice Quinn!" I shouted from the pier.

The chief just stood there and shook his head while the corpsman laughed.

"You're going to fit in just fine here, Quinn."

Sure, I fit in just fine, as long as I was buying the first round. Binge drinking while off the ship became commonplace for me.

I was traveling the world, visiting cities and places such as Hong Kong, Paris, Israel, Buckingham Palace, Bahrain, and Rome. But I have nothing to show for it, not one trinket to prove I was there, not one souvenir to place on my desk. I can't even recall many of those port calls. Instead of going sight-seeing like most people, I headed straight to the closest bar to drink. It was my way of having fun, relieving stress, dulling pain, and being "normal." I would stagger back to the ship with my drinking buddies and we'd all pass out in our bunks, often in our civilian clothes.

"Join the Navy and see the World!" I was seeing the world alright—through the bottom of a beer glass.

On board ship though, I was sober and very busy, but could sometimes squeeze in a chance to write a letter…

Phil,

Well, I am sitting at my battle station at General Quarters right now. I have a set of sound-powered phones on my head, listening to a fire drill being conducted on the other side of the ship and thought, what a great time to write Phil a letter.

Life on this floating time bomb is really a bitch. I now work twelve hours a day. Really! And I am also doing the Plan of the Day for the ship, which has to be done everyday. That is tough. Most of my time is spent doing that, but in two more weeks, I start rotating that duty with the other yeoman on a weekly basis.

One of our yeomen is getting out in thirty days. That will just put more workload on me. Oh well, who needs sleep anyway?

Phil, Hong Kong was great! We would have had a hell of a time together. It was a liberty port, so I only had to be on the ship once every four days! I took some really good pictures. The skyline is unreal. Ate my first shrimp cocktail the other day along with shark fin soup, turtle soup, even a snail and an oyster. Burger King and Big Macs were there also.

But I can't wait to get back to the States. That is really where it is for me. These foreign countries cannot compare. We pull into San Diego on 4 October.

I sent my Mom a box of goodies from Hong Kong. I got a ship's hat in there for you. It should come in two weeks. If I send you some pictures, will you start a photo album for me? Thanks.

Please write me at every opportunity. I don't care if it's a death threat on a brown paper bag, anything! Read this letter to my folks, okay? I am just too busy to write. I will try my best.

Well, back to work.

John

It is commonly said that the service brings out the best in a person. I agree. It also brings out the worst in some people.

Growing up, I was constantly being teased by other children about the way I walked, ran, or threw a baseball. I tried not to give their sharp comments much thought; usually I gritted my teeth and tried harder. Sometimes, when the taunts turned to threats of violence, my brothers stepped in and took care of business on my behalf. Anyone who picked on me learned that there were consequences.

During my first year in the Navy, the name calling returned with a vengeance. This time, my brothers were not around to help me when a bully decided to make me his target.

"Hey, Quinn, what the hell is wrong with you?" asked my tormentor. "You look like a freak or something!"

A co-worker in the captain's office, this farm boy from Kansas stood well over six feet tall and weighed close to 250 pounds. He had wild red hair and a temper to match.

Everyone on the ship seemed to step aside when they saw him coming down the passageway. As a seaman, he outranked me and used this fact to make my life miserable.

"Hey, Quinn, get out here and sweep up the passageway again. It looks like hell."

"Hey, Peg Leg, I don't feel like working today. You type up this report."

My first response to these comments was to ignore them. I didn't want to give him the satisfaction of getting a reaction out of me. My time on the wrestling mat had taught me mental as well as physical discipline and I used that knowledge to stay under control.

Then the taunts got physical. I would get punched in the arm as I stood in ranks for inspection or slapped in the back of my head while sitting at my desk typing. Not wanting to get in trouble for fighting, I did nothing. The assaults escalated.

"Quinn, I am going to hurt you bad one day," he threatened.

"What are you: some kind of baby? Fight me back! I would love for you to take a swing, Quinn!"

"You're a wimp, Quinn. Look at you: all skin and bones. I think I will just push you overboard one dark, moonless night when your back is turned. It would be hours before anyone even realized you were gone. Yup, I think that's the perfect plan to get rid of you."

Now afraid for my life, I finally went to the ship's executive officer (XO) for help.

"Come on now, Quinn. He is just teasing you. He doesn't mean anything by it."

"But sir, I'm being smacked and punched almost every day."

The XO chuckled. "Hell, sailor, that's just considered horseplay on board this ship. Now get back to work and quit wasting my time."

The bully was in the office one day, carrying on as usual when I finally reached my limit. I rose up out of my chair and walked toward the door.

"Where are you going, baby: running home to your mommy?"

"Not today!"

I locked the office door and picked up a nearby heavy dogging wrench.

"Let me show you how we do things in Detroit."

Ten minutes later, I unlocked the door and stepped out, wiping some blood from my uniform.

The bully from Kansas never teased me again. My brothers and Dad would have been proud.

"There he is! I see him!"

I heard the messenger of the watch shout as I walked toward the *Point Defiance*, ready to start my morning. The *Point D* was being retired and in the process the crew had been moved off the ship into government barracks located on base about a mile away. Some guys grumbled about having to walk to the ship, but I didn't mind. It felt good to stretch my legs a bit.

"Hey, Quinn!" The messenger shouted to me as I walked up the ship's steep entryway, or brow, with my shipmates.

"What the hell does he want?" I grumbled. "I'll be on board in a second."

"Hey, Quinn, your dad died last night!"

I froze in my tracks. What did he just say? What about Dad? My father is fine; there's nothing wrong with him. I'd just received his latest letter on Friday.

Knocking sailors out of my way, I sprinted up the remaining steps and grabbed the watchstander by the shoulders, squeezing hard enough to make him wince.

"What did you say about my dad? You're lying!"

"No, I was on watch when the ship got the Red Cross message this morning."

By this time, the senior watchstander, the officer of the deck, came over and put his arm around my shoulders. "Quinn, I've been instructed to escort you up to the executive officer's stateroom."

"This guy just told me that my dad died last night, sir. Is this true?"

I looked at him with tears in my eyes.

"What! The messenger told you?"

"Is it true?"

"Oh my God, Quinn, I'm so sorry you had to find out this way. Yes, your father died of a heart attack early this morning. I am so very sorry."

My dad was dead. He was 51. I fell to my knees and sobbed.

I pushed it out of my mind as much as I could, keeping myself busy with work, but I couldn't do that for long...

Hi Pal,

What the heck is going on? Thanks for your letter. You know I enjoy hearing from you.

Phil, I really feel bad. Today my dad has been dead for six months. Dead. Shit. Phil, I can't believe it. Honest. Is this right? I mean, it seems like six days! I think it's all caught up to me, finally realizing what has happened. I've tried to not think about it, get absorbed in my work and that has helped—until now. Images keep flashing back to me, about hearing the news, the flight home, seeing everybody. It really screws with my head. At night is the worst. I just get to thinking about all the good times that I had with my dad and I could cry.

How is my brother Jim handling it? Does he talk to you at all? At least he has the family and friends to talk to. I have to write my feelings down. Man, don't let anyone read this, but if I don't do this, write my feelings down, I am going to go up a wall...

Christmas is going to be a trip. I am really looking forward to it, but Dad was such a positive force for the holidays, especially for Joe. God, I worry about him. What is he going to be like when he grows up? He and Dad were inseparable, you know that. I don't think he realizes what has happened. Kathy either.

117

Hey, I really appreciate this, Phil. I owe you one. I will see you when the snow flies.

I feel better.

John

After being on board the *Point Defiance* for almost nine months, I looked up from the pile of paperwork one day and saw the ship's career counselor standing in the doorway with a steaming mug of coffee in his massive hands.

"Seaman Quinn, you have received transfer orders."

"I'm being transferred, Chief?"

I was shocked. I knew the ship was scheduled to be retired soon, but having been in the Navy for just a year, and the *Point D* my first ship, I didn't fully understand what that could mean to my career.

"Where am I headed?"

I was in awe of the man. He never seemed to sleep, he drank coffee by the gallon in a cup that hadn't been washed since World War II, and he had more tattoos than the toughest biker. He had seen it all, done it all. I hoped to be just like him one day.

"What did I tell you about asking questions, Quinn?"

"You told me to keep my mouth shut and listen to the chief."

"Damn, kid, you're going to become admiral one day. You want to know where you are being transferred to, do you?"

"Yes, Chief."

"You are going to be a plank owner of SEAL Team THREE."

"What kind of a ship is that?"

"Say that again, Quinn. I can't believe you said that!"

"What kind of a ship is SEAL Team THREE?"

"Quinn, you are a classic. Broke the mold when they made you, that's for sure. Son, SEAL Team THREE ain't no ship. It's the Navy special forces, the frogmen."

"Really? I've never heard of them."

The chief explained that the Navy SEALs (short for Sea, Air, Land) were considered to be the most elite special forces unit in the entire world. Highly trained in all aspects of warfare, Navy SEALs use stealth, extreme physical toughness, and intelligence to conduct dangerous missions.

"What really sets these warriors apart from their counterparts in the Army or Marine Corps is the ability to strike from, and return to, the sea," he said with a glint in his eye. "Frogmen, as they are called, can swim great distances to a specific target, silently slip out of the ocean, conduct a mission, and smoothly glide back into the water without being noticed. No other unit in the world has this capability," he added.

They were the "baddest" of the bad. And now I was going to be stationed with them! He could see that I was getting excited.

"Now, Quinn, these are a special set of orders, and I got them for you because I like you, but remember: you are an administrative guy, not a SEAL. You're going to do their paperwork for them, not jump out of airplanes and run around some foreign jungle; so keep your mouth shut, work hard and remember, you ain't no snake eater."

Soon after, I packed up my sea bag, said my goodbyes and jumped into a taxi, making the short trip from Naval Station, 32nd Street, San Diego, where all the surface ships are moored, to Naval Amphibious Base, Coronado, official home of the Navy SEALs.

Approaching the special warfare complex, the taxi driver asked me where I wanted to be dropped off.

"Well, I am being assigned to SEAL Team THREE. Just drop me off at the entrance to their building."

"Sailor, I have never heard of that unit, and I've been driving a taxi for 20 years in Coronado."

Seeing a sign for SEAL Team ONE, I instructed the driver to let me out. I paid him and exited the taxi with all my worldly possessions in my sea bag and boot-camp issued blue plastic garment bag. Walking onto the quarterdeck of SEAL Team ONE, I looked at the watchstander guarding the place. He wore a gold insignia on his chest that resembled the logo for Budweiser beer. I'd never seen anything like it.

"I am here to report to SEAL Team THREE," I said in my toughest voice.

The petty officer of the watch looked me square in the eye and said, "There is no SEAL Team THREE."

I pulled out my orders not only to show the watchstander, but also to double-check myself. *Could I have screwed this up already?*

We looked over my transfer orders together.

"Damn. It does say SEAL Team THREE."

A deep voice suddenly boomed from the far end of the hall, "Did I hear someone is checking into my team?" Looking down a long hallway, I saw a large man on crutches coming toward me. He had on a green T-shirt, brown canvas shorts, and a jungle boot on one foot.

"Who are you?"

"I am Yeoman Quinn, sir. Here to report into SEAL Team THREE."

"Well, Quinn, consider yourself checked in. I am the XO of Team THREE and you are officially the third person assigned to the unit."

"Thank you, sir."

"I have one question for you, Quinn. Do you like to exercise?"

"No, sir, not really."

The large man laughed.

"Wrong answer, sailor, but I like your honesty. I will see you out on the grinder in ten minutes for PT."

With that, the executive officer turned and quickly made his way back down the hallway.

Turning to the watchstander, I asked, "Is he for real? He has a fresh cast on his leg, for Christ's sake!"

"You bet. The XO is a fitness machine and has been looking for someone to work out with all morning. Great timing, dude."

What? Nobody told me about this. Don't they know that I'm not a SEAL? Oh, my God. What about my legs? This is crazy! I'm the paperwork guy. Shit! Shit! Shit!

Ten minutes later, I was on the back parking lot doing push-ups with a Navy SEAL. The kid with cerebral palsy who could not do a duck walk two years ago, working out with one of the fittest military men on the planet…

Phil, what the heck, over?

Thought I would take the time and drop you a line and see how life is turning out.

I ran six miles today. A nice pace of eight minutes a mile. My knees are killing me. Running on pavement screws them up. Pow! Pow! Pow! I sound like a Mack truck.

Work has been tough. This paperwork burns you out. It never seems to stop.

Speaking of stopping (pretty smooth, huh?), not much else going on. Tell everyone I said hello.

Later – John

"Petty Officer Quinn, do you have that evaluation typed up and ready to go for me yet?" barked the large XO.

"Yes, sir. Please check your in-box."

"Hell, you are fast! How about that award that I need sent over to headquarters?"

"I'll have it for you in a minute, sir."

"Great! Can you hand deliver it on your mail run?"

"No problem. I'll leave here shortly."

When people hear that I was stationed with the Navy SEALs, they automatically think I was a SEAL: me, the skinny kid who failed his initial enlistment physical. I didn't go through basic underwater demolition school (BUDS), the grueling nine-month school that produces SEALs. I never learned to jump out of airplanes, swim underwater planting explosives, or navigate my way out of a jungle.

But I can type—and damn fast.

And that was exactly the reason I was assigned to SEAL Team THREE: to do their paperwork. SEAL Team THREE was the first naval special warfare team in history to have non-SEALs assigned to the unit from its inception.

We were called support personnel, regular sailors who handled the day-to-day operation of the team. No longer did these elite, athletic military machines have to type evaluations, order supplies, or pick up the command mail. Those mundane functions were turned over to sailors with fleet experience, which allowed the frogmen to concentrate fully on the job that they were trained to do.

To be assigned to the team was one thing, to earn their trust and confidence was another. It was a lot of hard work, but the payoff was huge. I wasn't a strong physical specimen, but I proved my worth by smoothly taking care of their tiny headaches.

And I was learning a valuable lesson, one that I would use for the remainder of my career. Being the best at my job took the focus off my physical symptoms.

"Hey, Quinn. I've got a problem with my paycheck. Can you tell me what the deal is?"

"John, I really need this award typed up today for one of my guys who's leaving tomorrow. Can you put some words together if I give you the details? Thanks, pal."

No matter what I was doing, I always made time to help these frogmen. I quickly learned that your word was your bond. If I said I was going to fix a pay problem, I'd resolve it. If someone needed to get a requisition signed by the commanding officer, I'd see that it found its way to the top of the captain's in-box.

The SEALs were happy knowing that the details of their naval careers were being taken care of by a sailor who cared about their problems. Being a man of my word quickly earned their trust, and trust was a powerful ally in the close-knit world of the SEALs.

"Thanks, Quinn. If there is anything that I can do for you, just let me know," was a comment I heard often. When a SEAL tells you that, he means it. That phrase told me that I had earned their trust and confidence.

However, there was another arena where I needed to prove myself in order to truly rise to a position of respect on the team.

"All right! Everyone circle up for PT!" yelled a first-class boatswain's mate.

Physical training is the life's blood of a Navy SEAL. Being in top condition lets them perform their duties at the highest levels. They can't slip out of shape or there are consequences. A SEAL depends on the members of his platoon to stay physically and mentally sharp at all times with no exceptions. Bottom line: if they get out of shape, people die.

So each morning after muster, the morning meeting, everyone would circle up on the grinder to exercise, SEAL team style—everyone. If I wasn't out there, that fact was noticed and dealt with quickly. I learned that immediately upon my arrival.

"Hey, Quinn, where in the hell were you this morning? Sitting on your butt behind that desk? I better see you out there right next to me tomorrow in the push-up position!" ordered the commanding officer.

After that, I rarely missed PT (since apparently my absence was more conspicuous than my clumsiness).

During these workouts, one SEAL was placed in the middle of a circle, calling out exercises, one right after another in the warm Coronado sunshine. The frogman who had this duty was considered the fittest SEAL on the team. To lead the team in exercise was considered a great honor.

"25 four-count jumping jacks. Ready! Begin!"

And the morning would start.

"Flutter kicks. Ready! Begin!"

"Eight-count body builders. Ready! Begin!"

After a grueling hour of morning calisthenics, the team headed out the back gate and sprinted north along Coronado beach for a quick four-mile run: quick for them; slow, steady and more than a bit embarrassing for me.

Unfolding a cheap lawn chair is like me running: I'm all over the place. My left leg swings out wildly when I stride, like there's a hinge on the outside of my left knee. My lower torso has a mind of its own. I also over pronate, or run on the outside of my left foot. I hunch forward, trying to find my center of gravity and, as a result, my shoes wear out in abnormal places. Both of my feet are also unusually flat. When they strike the pavement, they create a slapping sound like a wet towel being thrown. Whack! My feet absorb the entire weight of my body. I've been told you can hear me coming from a mile away!

It's not just my legs either. When I stride, my left arm does not swing naturally. It stays in place. That relates to the right-sided paresis noted on my childhood medical records. My adult running style is more like rocky road instead of smooth silk. People actually wince when they see me run. SEALs were no exception.

Shuffling along the Coronado beach brought forth the usual comments I had been hearing all my life.

"Damn, Quinn, you sure have an unusual stride!"

"Are you okay there, Quinn? Looks like you're hurting."

I'd deflect these remarks by telling the frogmen that I was hurt in boot camp, and the comments faded with time. It was just accepted that this was the way Quinn ran. The team bond was such that they would not allow anyone outside of SEAL Team THREE to make any wisecracks about my appearance. My buddies had my back.

"You better shut your mouth about Quinn; he's doing his best," I overheard my teammates say on many occasions. I appreciated the gesture and just kept showing up every morning, ready to do my best.

To say that I struggled while exercising with the SEALS was an understatement. I felt as if I were back on the wrestling mat, just trying to remain on the team. At first I could barely run one mile in the soft beach sand, and completed about ten push-ups while these Navy warriors cranked out 200. It made me feel very small.

One day, I bemoaned my feelings to my roommate.

"John, let me explain something to you," he told me as we relaxed in our barracks. "Just the fact that you're out there on the grinder exercising with us means a great deal. So what if you cannot do all the repetitions, or have to take a longer break between calisthenics. We just ask that you give one hundred percent effort."

"But I want to be able to keep up with everyone else."

"You don't understand, John. Most of us have been doing this for years. It's our way of life. We have to stay in shape as part of our job. You are a fleet sailor, and have only been here a short while. We are the most physically fit people in the world and you are right there with us, busting your butt. The guys see how hard you're working. Believe me. It's being noticed. Just keep showing up on the grinder and don't get so down on yourself."

So that's exactly what I did. Just like that year down in the basement, I kept at it, one push-up at a time. Although the daily exercise and running slowly improved my strength and endurance, pain was still my constant companion. I wasn't certain I would be able to continue, but I was as determined as any true SEAL.

They were machines, pushing their bodies seemingly without thought. Pain was just weakness leaving their bodies. They seemed to embrace it, welcome it. I asked my roommate about this ability to deal with physical pain. I wanted in on this secret.

"Ahhh, now you are asking the right questions, John. The answer is here," he said tapping my temple. "If you want to get rid of pain, you must put it away."

"What do you mean, 'put it away'?"

"Take your pain and put it in a large steel box with a strong lock."

This was a concept that I had never thought of before, one that I could possibly use to manage the everyday pain of my cerebral palsy.

"It's called compartmentalization, and it can be very effective. Just put pain away in your mind where no one can touch it."

I had learned a powerful lesson, one that I started to use immediately and still utilize today. I live in constant pain, particularly in my lower back. It feels as if a giant hand has taken hold of my hip socket and is squeezing unmercifully.

Now that I am out of the military, I could go to the doctor tomorrow and get some type of pill to ease my suffering. Prescription medicine has its place, but it's just not for me. Having learned with some difficulty that I have an addictive personality, I rarely even take aspirin. I prefer to use the strength of my mind, taught to me by my SEAL friend. So every morning I get up and mentally put pain away in my mind. That strong metal box and I have been through a lot together. Although it's been tested countless times by the smooth safecracker, Mr. Pain, it's not often unlocked.

I worked with the SEALs from April 1983 to October 1985 and considered the time spent there an honor. It was one of the most important tours of my career. I learned much about my body and mind, while gaining valuable experience in the world of naval administration.

Although I still felt a crippling shyness in many social situations, the team camaraderie began to work its magic on my self-esteem and confidence far better than drinking at the club. My bar nights tapered off. I was becoming recognized and valued as a hard-working, extremely professional young man.

The morning before I left SEAL Team THREE, I was on the grinder, in my usual spot, ready for morning exercise when the SEAL who normally was in the middle of the circle came over to me.

"Hey, Quinn, you want to lead us in PT today?" he asked.

"It would be my pleasure," I said, beaming.

I slowly moved to the middle of the circle. Looking around, I noticed all the SEALs making eye contact with me, nodding their heads in approval. I nodded back in silent thanks.

"Twenty-five, four-count jumping jacks!... Ready!... Begin!" I shouted, with tears in my eyes.

Keeping my secret about cerebral palsy was a challenge that I faced every day of my naval career. Every morning I woke with the constant dread that today would be the day my secret would be revealed, and I had many close calls.

I played the scene of how my Navy career would end over and over in my mind. My supervisor would escort me to a formal conference room where my entire chain of command was seated behind the most imposing, large oak desk.

"All right, sailor, the time for lying is over," the Captain would say. "We are here to get some answers and we want them right now. How long have you been deceiving the government?"

"What do you mean, sir?"

"Quit fooling around, Quinn. We know all about the cerebral palsy. What, did you think we wouldn't find out about it sooner or later? We have documentation right here that you checked the "no" box in the recruiter's office. We are set to process you out of the Navy on the grounds of false enlistment. The military does not want or need *someone like you*."

These were the nightmarish thoughts I carried each day of my career. I was so afraid of the Navy finding out about my secret that I stayed away from *all* doctors, civilian or military, even if I had routine issues such as sinus infections or the flu, for fear that they would start asking questions. I wanted no one to notice my eyes, feet, legs, hips, spine or any other physical defect. If just one civilian medical professional examined my body thoroughly, ran tests and made chart notes accordingly, I worried it would somehow end up on a records database and the Navy would not only pronounce me disabled and discharged immediately, but possibly indict me for lying about it.

To keep my secret safe, I did not seek help from a chiropractor, even while home on leave. I did not request pain medication, anti-inflammatory medicines, or muscle relaxants. I lived each day with pain and fear of discovery. I had gotten lucky during the hospitalization while I was in boot camp, and knew each day the challenge continued. It felt like the ultimate game of cat and mouse, a game upon which I bet my entire career.

Not only did I have to hide my symptoms, constantly keeping my thoughts on how I walked or ran every waking hour, I also had to overcome another major obstacle.

Finally executing a perfect duck walk and passing the physical that allowed me entrance into the military was a huge weight off my shoulders, but now in October 1985, that same weight returned. When I raised my right hand and swore an oath to support and defend the Constitution of the United States, my commitment lasted four years. To stay in the Navy and reenlist for another hitch would require a retaking of the physical, with the real possibility that I would fail and be sent home in shame.

Until now, I had banished that thought from my mind.

So I had a decision to make: Do I leave the service at the end of my four-year enlistment, safe in the knowledge that I accomplished something pretty extraordinary, or do I put it all on the line and try to serve another tour? My pride and lack of life options made the choice for me. I chose to gamble it all.

But *could* I pass another physical? There was only one way to find out.

"Petty Officer Quinn, I want you to get off the examination table and walk across the room for me," said the medical officer of SEAL Team THREE, where I was stationed.

Hell. He must suspect something.

I quickly ran through a checklist in my mind. Where had I screwed up?

With a forced calm, I hopped down and stood as straight as possible, slowly making my way across the cold tile floor.

My mom would've been proud: Heel and toe every time.

The doctor was not so easily fooled. "Get back on the table and lie on your back," he ordered sharply.

Here it comes, I thought. The jig is up. I'm about to be sent home.

The SEAL doctor looked closely at my hip and spinal alignment. He probed my left shoulder with his fingers and examined the muscular development of my legs. He told me to sit up and examined both of my eyes carefully.

Seeing me sweat, he asked, "Are you nervous, Petty Officer Quinn?"

"No, sir."

Yeah, right. I was almost quaking with fear. If this doctor said I was unfit to reenlist, that was it. My military career was over.

"Hmm." That was the only sound he made.

Finishing his examination, he went to a huge medical reference book that sat on his desk, rapidly flipping through the pages, stopping when he found what he was looking for. After what seemed like an eternity, he said, "Are you keeping something from me?"

"No, sir." I held my breath.

He stared at me without saying a word for almost a full minute. I could see that he was struggling with his decision. Finally, he spoke.

"Okay. If you want to serve your country for another four years, I'm not going to hold you back."

"Thank you, sir." I could barely get the words out.

"Just don't make me regret my decision, son. Continue to work hard and make something of yourself. Good luck in the rest of your career."

With that, the Navy SEAL doctor winked and walked away.

He must have known about my cerebral palsy and was letting me reenlist anyway. I could breathe again. *I'll be damned!*

8

Career Progression

My first reenlistment began with a long cross-country trip from the SEAL Team THREE based in Coronado, California to my next assignment, shore duty at the United States Central Command , located at MacDill Air Force Base, Florida.

What was a Navy guy doing on an Air Force base? USCENTCOM is what is referred to as a joint command, with various military branches of service working together under one roof. CENTCOM's area of responsibility extends to 27 countries in the Middle East, East Africa, and Central Asia. This powerful coalition has been the main American presence in numerous operations, including the Persian Gulf War, the United States war in Afghanistan, and the 2003 invasion of Iraq.

I was unpacking my sea bag and getting settled into my new barracks room when an old friend poked his head thru the door.

"Well, look who's here!"

Bill and I had crossed paths a few months earlier in the summer of 1985 on a military exercise in Egypt called Bright Star. He was on the CENTCOM staff which ran the event, a massive affair, while I was tasked to administratively support the Navy SEALs. I was impressed with the commitment to excellence I saw during my time in the desert and thought if I had the chance, I'd like to work with these professionals. I had gotten my wish; we were all on the same team now.

"Hey, John, it's really great to see you. Welcome to beautiful Tampa."

Bill walked quickly into my room to shake hands.

"Thanks. It's good to be here."

After the heart-stopping experience of passing my reenlistment physical, that phrase was not just lip-service, I meant it most sincerely. It *was* good to still be in the Navy. "My SEAL Team chief laughed when I told him that I wanted to be transferred to CENTCOM. He said it was considered pretty demanding shore duty and actually tried to talk me out of it."

I should have listened to the chief.

Headed up by a four-star Marine general, CENTCOM was divided into six directorates, each having a specific function: Administrative, Intelligence, Operations, Logistics, Plans and Policy, and Communications. It was like a huge tree with each directorate a massive limb.

I was assigned to the Political-Military Branch of the Plans and Policy directorate. In military speak; it was referred to as J-5 Pol-Mil.

Within the Pol-Mil branch, there were 18 Action Officers (AOs) who were responsible for monitoring the political and military events in certain parts of the world. One AO would be in charge of everything going on in Egypt, another Saudi Arabia, and so on. They would closely monitor elections results, track intelligence findings, and try to put their fingers on the pulse of the people. If an AO found something in his study he thought important, he would put his findings in a fact paper and submit them for review by the chain of command.

Everything had to be typed. Bulging trip books filled with country facts or detailed itineraries would be required by various generals or admirals at a moment's notice. Thick summary reports needed to be created detailing the latest world crisis. Briefing slides would be requested immediately for a meeting with the latest visitor from Washington, D.C., such as the Secretary of Defense or the American Ambassador to Kuwait. It was non-stop, critical, time-sensitive paperwork.

Stationed at SEAL Team THREE, I rarely saw classified material and had ample time to plan out my day. At MacDill, everything I touched was classified secret or above, and needed to be handled with urgency. I had only one enlisted typist to assist me in keeping pace with the needs of 18 high-ranking officers, all of whom had the same approach to my desk.

I was usually pounding the word processor and I always got the same leading question, "Petty Officer Quinn, what are you working on?"

My answer was always the same, "Put it on the pile."

My in-box seemed to grow overnight with massive projects: one-hundred-fifty page embassy evacuation plans, thick operational guidelines which outlined the next big military operation, and vital radio messages needing the general's signature.

Everyone's needs were important.

As I worked, I'd often stop and realize that I had come a long way from *USS Point Defiance*. In just over three years I had gone from being low man on the totem pole to being a petty officer and the guy that people turned to when they wanted something done fast, accurate and right. I took a lot of pride in my work and was soon recognized for my efforts with glowing performance evaluations that stated:

"His maturity, initiative, and can-do spirit allow him to accomplish tasks normally assigned to commissioned officers..."

"In all aspects, he is a dedicated, conscientious, and motivated sailor..."

"His performance has been outstanding in an environment of long hours, high security classification, and time sensitive issues..."

Hell, I was even nominated for Sailor of the Year by the Tampa Navy League!

I was 24 years old.

Acutely aware that the documents I was working on might be seen by the President of the United States, I felt tremendous pressure at work. This internal stress manifested itself physically with a return of those classic cerebral palsy symptoms: muscle spasticity, rigidity, and fatigue.

I performed well under the burden of shifting deadlines, but my body and mind paid a price. I'd often get back to the barracks and collapse on my bed, my body racked with the pain of sitting at a computer for twelve long hours. My back would spasm and my legs shake.

I couldn't go to the base doctor and say, "Hey doc, you have anything you can give me for cerebral palsy?" That secret was mine to keep. My mind raced, still focused on "that" document waiting for me on my desk. I lay awake at night, unable to relax my screaming muscles and frantic mind despite the tiredness I felt.

Beer once again became my after-work medicine of choice. With the day's responsibilities met, my fellow administrative buddies and I would often get together in the barracks to drink and commiserate about our day. Although my alcohol consumption had tapered off at SEAL Team THREE, it served as the perfect remedy for the physical and emotional stress of CENTCOM. Ties were loosened and the beers poured.

Dressed in suits, we could have been Wall Street bankers discussing the latest stock deal, accountants worrying about April 15th, or car salesmen talking about the future of the auto industry.

But we were young enlisted men and women who had to prepare flawless, important military documents under crushing deadlines. It felt great to talk about the pressures of working in that climate with people who understood.

"Guys, you should've seen the piece of crap document the major handed me to work on today … of course it was hot …

"I had to prepare a travel book for the general's wife, for crying out loud!"

"The captain asked me what my plans were for tomorrow. I told him since tomorrow is Saturday, I plan to sleep, sir!"

We always laughed and that was good, the steam being released from our pressure cooker.

During the spring of 1987, I was granted some much-needed leave time from the pressures of MacDill. I went home to Michigan to spend some time with my family. It would be a trip that would forever change me.

In the pecking order of our family, my brother Steve was one year older than I, but fifty years advanced on the charm scale. With thick, dark hair and a mischievous grin inherited from our father, Steve had movie-star looks with the grace to match. When my brother walked into a room, every head turned in his direction.

A superb athlete, there wasn't a sport Steve couldn't master. At age 11, he played baseball with men almost twice his age. On the football field, he was the star running back. I would sit with Mom on Sunday afternoons and marvel at his moves on the gridiron.

He reminded me of the character Tom Cruise played in the movie *The Color of Money*, about a pool hustler. My brother could charm the skin off a snake. And women loved Steve. I went to a nightclub with him and a few friends when I came home from boot camp. At the end of the night, Steve told me to hold out my hands. Then he placed 15 little slips of paper into them. They were girls' phone numbers he had collected in the short time we were there.

Unfortunately, for all his charm, grace, and athletic skill, there was one area of his life that Steve did not find easy and that was following the rules. He liked to bend and even break them. In his mind, they didn't apply to him. Don't have the money to pay for something? Just take it. Don't feel like delivering the newspapers on your route? Throw today's edition in the dumpster. Feel like skipping class? Sure. Why not?

Drugs and alcohol began to play a starring role in his life and clouded Steve's judgment further. With a wink and a grin, he could get out of most predicaments faster than Houdini, but life has a way of catching up with you.

And it was already nipping at Steven's heels.

My brother Steve, during his time at sea in the Navy. That gun mount he is standing next to is the one that he was responsible for.

He had dropped out of high school his senior year, messed around for a while, and, perhaps to find some direction and purpose in his life, joined the Navy. For a guy who didn't like to stay within the lines of society, the military seemed like a strange choice, but Steve was out of options.

In his apprenticeship school, Steve was a gunner's mate, responsible for the safe and accurate firing of the gun mounts on board Navy ships. Unfortunately, he was learning more than how to expend ordnance. He was getting in serious trouble for drinking, fighting, and worse. When he returned one time from being AWOL, hung over with knuckles bruised and bloody, his wit and charm did not work on Navy officials, who tossed him into the brig. As the disciplinary problems escalated, they threw him out of the Navy altogether.

With his bad conduct discharge, my brother's role as the "black sheep" within our family was now stronger than ever, a role that Steve embraced, regardless of the impact it had on those who loved and cared about him. My parents spent many a sleepless night worrying about where their errant son was and what he was doing. Their concerns put a great strain on everyone in the house.

When I came home on leave, Steve seemed to have his life turned in the right direction. He had finally found work as a landscaper and had begun dating a nice girl whose mother was a real estate agent. She helped Steve buy a small house and he seemed to be settling into suburban life. But my brother's outward appearance only served to hide the demons that were struggling inside.

Since I was in the military and only able to come home to visit twice a year, I was unaware that Steve was now relying heavily on drugs and alcohol to get through each day. On the last Sunday of my vacation, the family gathered at Mom's house for Easter dinner. I sat in Dad's place and felt honored and sad at the same time. I enjoyed catching up on everyone's life and was pleased that Steve seemed unusually happy and upbeat. As the ham and meatballs were being passed around the table, I asked my brother for a favor.

"Hey, Steve, I was wondering if you'd like to go shopping soon and help me buy a good baseball mitt. Mine is too small and I want to play softball down at MacDill."

Steve looked at me and grinned. "Sure, John. Let's go tomorrow and pick you out a winner."

The next day, he took me to the local sporting goods store and schooled me on what to look for in a quality glove. After looking over several models, we both came to the conclusion that a Rawlings mitt was the best choice for me. We made plans to come back later in the week and pick it up.

On Wednesday night, my siblings and I, Phil, and two other buddies met at our favorite bar for dinner and a few drinks, something we always did whenever I was in town. It was a great time, full of fun and laughter. I sat there thinking how special it was to have everyone together, smiling and getting along.

Steve, who was sitting across from me, sensed it as well. Several times during the night he would look around at everybody, not saying much, just sitting back in his chair and soaking it all in.

Finally, he leaned close and, motioning me to do the same, shouted over the blare of the jukebox, "You are going to make a fine chief one day, John."

I was stunned. I currently held the rank of second-class petty officer, a far cry from the exalted level of chief.

"Me? A chief? No way in hell, Steve," I blurted. "That's a long way off and I can't even dream that big."

Steve did not seem phased by my comment.

"Heck, John, I bet you make master chief. In fact I would carve it in stone."

My big brother leaned back in his chair, crossed his arms and just smiled at me. Master chief petty officer is the highest enlisted rank in the Navy.

"You're pulling my leg now. There is no way that I will *ever* be considered for something like that."

"Yes, you will, and I want you to remember who told you first," he said, a big grin on his face.

Those were the last words he ever said to me.

He left the bar a few hours later and went home. Early that morning, in his kitchen, he killed himself with his shotgun.

On his kitchen table, still in the box, sat a brand new Rawlings softball mitt.

What do you say to someone whose brother just committed suicide? I learned that people have difficulty finding the right words, or any words at all. One of the first calls I made after Steve's death was to my military boss, an Army colonel.

I sat on the porch of my Mom's house when I called him. The late April wind blew cold.

"Hi there, Petty Officer Quinn. This is a surprise," the colonel said. "How's the leave going?"

"Not too well, sir."

"What's going on?"

"My brother killed himself this morning."

Silence. The phone line sounded as empty as my emotions.

Hell, I was still in shock.

"Damn, Quinn. Are you okay? Anything I can do for you?"

"Well, sir, I am going to have to extend my leave so I can be here for the funeral. That should be sometime later this week."

"Sure, John, take as much time as you need."

"Thank you, Colonel."

"No problem. I will take care of that extension personally. And we'll just keep your brother's passing between you and me right now. When you get back, you can handle it however you think is best."

Great. Another secret to add to my growing list of secrets. *Thanks, brother.*

It turned out the colonel was right: people didn't want to hear the entire truth.

Who wants to hear how I sat with the Yellow Pages on my lap calling local maid services hoping to find one who would make the blood and gunk on that kitchen wall go away?

"Sunshine Maid Service, how may I help you?"

"Yes, I have a problem and I was hoping you would be able to help me or direct me to someone who could."

"What's your problem, sir?"

"Well, my brother took his life this morning and there is some blood and brain…"

She hung up before I could finish the sentence. At least she didn't laugh like the people at several other places that I had called earlier.

Shaking my head in frustration, I was slowly coming to the realization that my brothers and I would have to clean up Steven's mess ourselves.

How do you explain to people how it felt to go into the hardware store to buy buckets, sponges, rubber gloves, and pine oil knowing what you're going to use them for?

"Golly, you guys getting ready to do some spring cleaning?" asked the too-cheerful checkout clerk while ringing up a mop and bucket.

"Yup," said Michael without missing a beat.

How do you explain all that to outsiders?

When I returned to the base, coworkers came up to me and asked me the same question. "How was your vacation, John?"

What was I going to tell them? That my brother Steve blew the back of his head out in his kitchen?

"Okay" was the only thing people wanted to hear.

The lie rolled smoothly off my tongue. But things were not okay. I buried myself in my work, coming in early and staying late. I wanted to be around people, but at the same time I wanted to be left alone. I felt I had a sign on my back that said, "This guy's brother committed suicide."

My emotions were mixed, turbulent, but the strongest was anger.

White-hot anger directed squarely at Steven.

Here I was, a skinny kid with all the grace of a box of rocks who struggles to make it through the day with a body that hurts with every step and has to keep the handicap a secret.

Steven was born with good looks, charm, and a smoothness of stride. And *he* is the one who checks out, takes the easy road, leaving his family and friends to come up with the answers. It just wasn't fair.

Steve was a quitter, who would have guessed? The more I thought about it, the angrier I got.

I often paced the floor of my barracks room, at night, alone with my thoughts and with my mind racing.

How dare he do this to our mother! To our entire family!

What problems were so bad that he had to kill himself?

Why didn't he just pick up the phone and call someone, anyone?

My mind danced with these questions and many, many more. The harder I tried to make sense of Steve's death, the faster I paced.

I was having trouble sleeping and was drinking more than usual. I couldn't concentrate at work and would snap at anyone who got too close. I felt like a piano wire being stretched tight. I tried to get help by attending a couple of support meetings for people whose family members had killed themselves, but to me, it was a bunch of people sitting around in a circle crying and feeling sorry for themselves. Everyone wanted to come up and give me a hug. What a bunch of pathetic losers. I had walked away in disgust.

Still not emotionally recovered from my father's death, the added burden of this horrific loss was sending me over the edge. I believed I was losing my mind. Something had to give before it was too late… I picked up the phone.

"Hillsborough County Crisis Hotline, my name is Dan, how can I help you tonight?"

"My brother killed himself a couple of months ago and I want to talk to someone."

"Sure, I can help you with that. Can I get your name so that we can begin?"

"My name is John."

"Okay, great, John. Why don't you start by telling me what happened to your brother?"

"Let me ask you a question first, sir."

"Sure, John, what's that?"

"Have you ever had a brother commit suicide before?"

"Ah, no, I haven't."

"Well, how in the hell can you help me if you haven't gone through the same experience yourself?" My knuckles turned white as I gripped the receiver.

Doesn't anybody understand?

The counselor was unfazed by my yelling. "Well, if you must know, I have a master's degree in counseling from the University of Maine and…"

"So I guess the answer is no, huh?" I said with as much sarcasm as I could muster.

"No, I haven't had a brother commit suicide, but I believe I can still help you."

What an idiot. I needed real help from someone who understood.

"Here's what I need, Dan. Go find me a counselor, someone whose brother has blown his head out with a shotgun, and get him or her on the phone. I'll hold."

141

"You *are* kidding, right?" The guy chuckled slightly as my anger grew by the second.

"Does it sound like I'm kidding, Dan?"

Something in my tone must have told him I was ready to shatter into a million pieces because he put me on hold. About ten minutes later, a lady came on the line.

"This is Joan, is this John on the line with me?"

"Yes, it is."

"Hi, John. Dan tells me that you wanted to talk to someone whose brother has committed suicide, is that right?"

"Yeah, you see my brother killed himself and I wanted to talk with someone who could relate with what I've been going through."

"Well, I can understand that, my brother also took his life."

"Really?" I slumped in my chair, the coiled tension in my body melting instantly.

"Yes, he did. Now why don't you tell me about your brother?"

"Well, you see, I am in the Navy and was home on vacation..."

Counseling proved to be my salvation. Over the next eighteen months I learned that Steven's choice had not been the "easy way out." My overwhelming grief and anger caused me to dismiss a wonderful support group, Survivors of Suicide, as a bunch of pathetic losers.

Many years later I also discovered that bipolar psychiatric disorder ran in our family, which may have also been a contributing factor in Steven's death. With the help of Joan, I learned that some secrets just aren't worth keeping.

Suicide Is Selfish, Says Someone Who Knows

By Karen Haymon Long

—*Tampa Tribune* Staff Writer

Tampa – John Quinn didn't cry when his brother killed himself. He hasn't cried since. But he hopes to redirect his sorrow by telling others about his ordeal. By sharing his story, he says, maybe something good will come from the horror. Maybe it could dissuade someone from doing what his older brother did.

Just a year apart, John and Steve Quinn grew up near Detroit in a close-knit Catholic family of eight children. They shared a bedroom, a passion for athletics, and a stubborn streak they inherited from their Detroit police officer dad.

They were brothers, but they were friends, too, and the friendship lasted into adulthood.

It ended two Easters ago, just a few days after John's 25th birthday, when Steve shot himself with his father's shotgun.

He was 26.

Now 26 himself, John Quinn recently told his story publicly for the first time during a Mental Health Association of Hillsborough County banquet. He says he hopes to speak to youth groups about his brother's suicide. He wants them to know how much suicide can hurt families and friends.

"It took me about a year to be even keel," says Quinn, who is in the Navy, stationed at MacDill Air Force Base. "I'm not angry anymore. It's more disappointment, and longing to talk to him."

Quinn, who wears his brown hair short even by military standards, says he changed drastically after Steve killed himself. He snapped at people for no reason. He was restless and angry all the time.

Finally, afraid his blind rage might jeopardize his job, he called the Hillsborough County Crisis Center Suicide and Crisis Line. A counselor—who asked to remain anonymous in this story – counseled him over the telephone, sometimes several times a week, for a year and a half.

She told him her brother killed himself, too, so she drew on her experience and counseling to help Quinn.

"I don't like to think what would have happened if I hadn't called," he says.

Coworkers who knew about his brother were sympathetic. But most said things such as, "It must be hard," or "I know it's tough," which he says didn't help much.

"I wanted someone who knew what I had been through. I was looking for someone to push me along, to say, "This is normal. I've been through this, and look where I have gotten. You are going to get to a point where you are going to be okay, too.""

His counselor did that. And she encouraged him to face his anger, to vent it in physical activity and not to be so hard on himself. He took up squash, hitting the nearly indestructible rubber balls so hard that he broke three or four, but the physical activity calmed his anguish.

One of the most important lessons she taught him was that something positive would come out of the tragedy, he says.

She was right. After hours of counseling and introspection, he says, he became less angry at coworkers and easier on himself. He learned to delegate work. It became easier for him to talk about his feelings and listen to others. His family grew closer, too, he says.

He'd had no clue his brother was thinking of suicide. But looking back now, he sees some signs. Steve dropped out of high school his senior year, joined the Navy, then quit that, too. After that, he was in and out of jobs as a construction worker and gardener. When he needed money, he sometimes borrowed from his family.

"He was frustrated," Quinn recalls. "Steve had a lot of pride in himself, and when he might have to settle for a little less right now, he didn't want to wait… drinking was a problem also."

Steve and their dad had had a falling out and were barely speaking when their dad died of a heart attack six years ago. His brother felt guilty about that, Quinn says.

"He thought he was a problem to my family. He thought it would be better if he wasn't here," Quinn says.

Quinn was home for Easter and to celebrate his birthday two years ago with his mother and all his brothers and sisters.

Steve told him then he noticed how well he was doing in his Navy career and that he would go far.

"He didn't say it in a jealous way. It was more like a goodbye," Quinn recalls.

Quinn says now he finds himself blocking out sad memories and tends to remember only the good. But he is not angry anymore—just sad sometimes.

That sadness shows when he talks about how his brother shot himself in his kitchen, about the incomprehensible note he left, about cleaning up the mess.

Counseling made the pain tolerable, he says, and he recommends it for anyone going through hard times. He says he doesn't think he could have gotten out of his depression alone.

"Damn it!" I shouted, slamming the phone down. I had just finished speaking with my detailer, the person in Washington, D.C. who arranges transfers. The detailer is contacted by naval personnel prior to the expiration of the four-year tour in order to see the availability of locations or assignments. Job slots, called requisitions, and openings, become available every month on a first-come, first-served basis.

It was March 1989 and I was nearing the end of my tour.

I had been stationed at USCENTCOM for almost four years. Combined with my tour with the Seals, it had been over six years since I'd been on board ship. After that length of shore duty, the Navy said it was time for me to get back to sea duty and sharpen my skills as a yeoman. For someone in my current job rating, sea duty was a 36-month stretch. I thought about my cerebral palsy secret and the numerous challenges I would face.

Could my body handle the physical demands of shipboard life? What about the mental strain of keeping my CP under wraps in such a closed environment? My only previous shipboard experience was on the *Point Defiance* just prior to its retirement, and that relatively short hitch had left me exhausted in mind, body, and spirit. How would I hold up for three long years?

I could try to get assigned to a small ship in a far corner of the world and maintain a low profile in order to fulfill the Navy's mandate. It would be taking the easiest road possible.

Sailors do it all the time, and I had good reason. But I didn't want to hide out on any old ship. My pride was on the line and outweighed my fears. In addition, my parents didn't raise me that way. They had always pushed me to be my best and not give up. I had joined the Navy against all odds, and I wouldn't back down from this challenge either. After a period of mental wrestling, I set aside my reservations and made my decision.

I wanted a battleship.

Re-commissioned by President Ronald Reagan, four battle-ships were in the Navy's fleet in the 1980s: the *USS Iowa*, the *USS New Jersey*, the *USS Missouri*, and the *USS Wisconsin*. Because of the overwhelming firepower of their 16-inch guns, unmatched speed and history dating back to World War II, these dread-naughts had quickly become the pride of the Navy. Every sailor wanted to serve on board and be known as a "battleship sailor." I was no exception.

Stationed with me at USCENTCOM was a Navy rear admiral who had actually served as the commanding officer of the *New Jersey*. I used to walk into his office on occasion just to gaze at the many pictures he displayed to commemorate his time on board. I thought this was the ship for me as I looked at the powerful 16-inch guns blazing away at a target in the distance.

However, getting orders seemed impossible. I had begun calling my detailer nine months prior to my transfer, and the conversation was pretty much the same each time.

"I need to get back to sea and want to serve on board a battleship."

"Petty Officer Quinn, I don't have any requisitions for battleships this month, but I do need sailors on a destroyer home ported in Jacksonville, Florida."

"No. I really want on a battleship. I'll call you again next month."

"Okay, but there are only four battleships, and I need sailors on other ships as well."

"Nope. I'll call you in a few weeks."

This back and forth went on for a total of six months with the same result: no battleships available. Finally, it was getting close to my transfer date. If I didn't finalize a set of orders this week, my detailer was going to send me where *she* needed me to go—not an appealing option.

I placed the call.

"Hi. This is Petty Officer Quinn and I'm just checking to see if any battleship assignments are available?" Perhaps the seventh time was the charm.

"Quinn, we've been down this road before. There are no openings in battleships. If you don't make a decision on the phone with me right now, I'm going to put you on a slow boat to China! You get my meaning?"

I slammed the phone down. "Damn it!"

A Marine colonel stepped out of his office to see what the noise was all about. "Quinnman, what the hell has got you all riled up?"

The colonel and I had worked closely together my entire tour at USCENTCOM, traveling from Fort Bragg, North Carolina to the Egyptian desert. He knew that if I was upset, there was a good reason.

"Colonel, I don't want to bother you. Sorry that I yelled, sir."

The colonel didn't need my petty troubles added to his already overburdened plate, but he was no ordinary Marine.

"Spit it out, son. That's an order."

Looking at the colonel, I knew he was serious.

"Colonel, you know that I'm up for transfer."

"Sure do. Back to sea duty if I remember correctly."

"Yes, sir. Well, I want orders to a battleship."

"Okay. Sounds great. So what's the problem?"

"My detailer says there are no battleship assignments available and has been telling me this for the past six months."

"You've been talking to her, trying to arrange this transfer on your own?"

"Yes, sir, and I'm to the point that if I don't choose something today, I am going to be placed on a slow boat to China."

"Is that what she said to you, Quinnman?"

"Yes, sir."

"Come with me."

I followed the colonel for a short walk down the hall. He knocked on the door of the former commanding officer of the *USS New Jersey* as we both entered the Admiral's office.

"Admiral, do you have a minute, sir?"

"Sure, Colonel. Come on in and have a seat," said the admiral, looking up from a pile of paperwork.

"You know Petty Officer Quinn, sir?"

"Sure do. How is everything going, Quinn?"

"Great, sir. Thank you."

"The colonel has nothing but praise for you, says you should have been a Marine," he said to me.

"That's high praise coming from the colonel, sir."

"Now, what can I do for you gentlemen?"

"Quinn here is up for orders, Admiral, and has it in his head that he wants to become a battleship sailor."

The admiral looked at me questioningly, "Is that true, Petty Officer? Do you think you have what it takes to become a battleship sailor?"

"Yes, sir."

I gulped as the admiral stared at me for a few long moments, searching my soul and sizing me up. Finally, he spoke.

"I don't think you have what it takes to serve on a battleship. I really don't."

I was stunned. *What? Are you kidding me? Don't have what it takes?*

The look on the admiral's face was stony and serious.

"Sir? I can do it. I know I can." I felt the old familiar mix of fear and guilt churning in my gut. It turned quickly to resentment. My leg started to twitch.

You're damn right, I can do it, Admiral. I am a damn good sailor.

"Look. Getting assigned to a battleship is no joke. Those ships deserve experienced sailors who know their way around the deck of a ship. How much sea time do you have, Petty Officer Quinn?"

"Nine months, sir, on board an amphibious ship, *Point Defiance*."

"Nine months sea time and you expect me to wave a magic wand to get you orders on board one of the world's finest warships?"

The two stars on the Admiral's collar seemed to glow more brightly by the moment.

My resentment was quickly escalating into anger, fueled in no small part by my own secret fears.

"I don't expect anything, Admiral. I have earned everything through plain hard work. I really don't care if you get me orders to a battleship or not, but if you do, I'll give it my best, just like I have my entire career."

Don't have what it takes, my ass! I've been hearing that my whole life.

I opened my mouth to say something else, words that I might have regretted. Then I heard a sound that made me turn my head.

The Marine colonel was sitting on the couch behind me, a huge smile on his face that turned into a large guffaw. The admiral followed suit, pounding the desk with his hand, his head shaking with laughter.

"What the heck is so funny, sirs?" I almost had to shout above the din.

My words made the two powerful men laugh even harder. The admiral's aide poked his head in the door to see what was going on. He looked at me for the reason, but I just shrugged my shoulders.

Slowly, it dawned on me what had just happened. I had been taken and I had bought it. It was like being back home getting needled by my brothers!

Finally able to speak, the colonel said, "Damn, Quinn. I thought you were going to punch the admiral in the nose!"

"That was classic, for sure. Haven't laughed that hard in years," The admiral wiped his eyes and finally got serious.

"The Colonel and I both know how hard you've worked here at CENTCOM, and I've got to tell you that if you show half as much spirit as you did talking to me just a second ago, you'll do just fine on a battleship."

Picking up the phone, the admiral inquired, "What's the number to your detailer?"

The paperwork approving my transfer to the *USS Iowa* arrived a week later. I was going to be a battleship sailor.

I had completed my CENTCOM duty and was on vacation until I reported to my next assignment. April 19, 1989 I was home in Michigan. I was just finishing up a lunch of peanut butter on fresh pumpernickel bread. With orders in hand to the *Iowa*, I was excited to finally get on board a battleship and begin the next phase of my naval career. After my leave, I would be walking the wooden decks of that historic ship.

The *USS Iowa* was particularly famous among battleships. It had served as the flagship for President Reagan during the nation's 210th birthday celebration, which included the centennial rededication of the Statue of Liberty in New York harbor.

With a big glass of milk in hand, I plopped down in Dad's recliner and grabbed the television remote to do a little mindless channel surfing. As I flipped through the stations, I caught CNN with *Breaking News.*

"We don't know the full extent of damage, as reports are just coming into us here at the newsroom," a long-haired anchor woman was saying, "But to recap, there has been some kind of explosion on board the U.S. Navy ship *Iowa...*"

As I anxiously listened, more details emerged and painted a grim picture. Something had gone horribly wrong on board the *Iowa* and sailors had died. An image of the battleship filled the screen as the news anchor gave a history of the ship.

"Commissioned again in April 1984, the *USS Iowa* is the lead ship of four *Iowa*-class battleships, with a crew of more than fifteen hundred..."

What about the crew? Is the ship still afloat? How many have been killed?

Mom came through the front door after a morning of grocery shopping. I hadn't heard the car pull up.

"Honey, can you help bring the groceries in... what's wrong, John?"

Looking at my mother snapped me out of my trance. I was gripping the remote control so tightly my knuckles had turned white. The glass of milk sat untouched and forgotten. "There's been an explosion."

"An explosion? Where?"

"Mom, please?"

"But, John, the groceries..."

"Sit down, Mom." Something in my voice told my mother this was serious.

She moved quietly to the couch, hugging her over-sized purse like a security blanket.

"There's been an explosion on the ship that I'll be reporting to in the next few weeks, the *USS Iowa.*"

"An explosion? The ship on television right now? That's *your* ship?"

"Yes, ma'am."

"Oh, John."

We both sat transfixed by the tragic events that were unfolding before our eyes. Reporters on location struggled with their emotions, rapidly delivering information as it became available.

"Initial reports estimate that as many as fifty sailors may have perished in an explosion that rocked the battleship's number two gun turret..."

Fifty sailors! Are they serious? Fifty sailors!

It had to be a large explosion to take out so many men. How many sailors manned a battleship turret?

"...The *Iowa* is currently conducting gunnery exercises off the coast of Puerto Rico. Pentagon officials report the warship is steaming back to its home port in Norfolk, Virginia under its own power..."

The phone rang. Mom jumped to answer it and handed the cordless handset quickly to me. It was my brother Michael. "John, are you watching the news?"

"Yes, sure am, Mike."

"That's the ship you have orders to?"

"Yes, it is."

"Damn. I feel kind of guilty for saying this, but I'm sure glad you haven't reported on board yet. Can you just imagine what those guys are going through?"

"I've been sitting here thinking that very thing. It must be terrible."

When the smoke cleared and the final numbers were tallied, it was revealed that 47 sailors had died.

Sitting in the safety of my childhood home, I felt trapped between two worlds. Partly I wanted desperately to be on that battleship to lend a helping hand where needed.

Being an administrator, I knew the mountain of detailed paperwork that the Navy required to document that staggering loss of life. An investigation would have to be prepared and statements given. The other part of me was glad that I had not yet reported on board, safe in the knowledge that it was just not my time.

When the casualty list of the victims was released, I saw that one of the sailors who died was from Michigan. Accompanied by my sister Janet, I, in dress blues, attended his funeral. It was a stark reminder to me that the world I was about to step back into, the one of a seagoing sailor, was fraught with danger, even in peacetime.

On June 6, 1989, six weeks after the worst peacetime accident in modern naval history, the *Iowa* sailed out of Norfolk to the Mediterranean Sea for a previously scheduled six-month deployment. The loss of 47 personnel, many of whom held key positions of leadership, would have crippled a lesser organization than the United States Navy.

Courtesy of the Naval History and Heritage Command

The USS Iowa

9

Love and Heartbreak

Women and a career in the Navy don't mix—at least for me. In the past I'd had little experience with the opposite sex, but now had enough bravado to talk to them.

It was the summer of 1991 and I was home in Garden City on vacation. Having completed a successful tour onboard Battleship *Iowa*, I was now assigned to the guided missile destroyer *USS Chandler*, docked out of San Diego. Just returning from a Persian Gulf deployment, I stopped into a bar one night to grab a beer and noticed a couple of cute girls talking with some civilian. Something they said caught my attention, so I ordered a Michelob and tuned into the conversation.

"...Went down to Ft. Bragg to welcome the troops home from the war; just drove there on the spur of the moment," explained one girl.

"Yeah, we didn't have a place to stay or anything. We thought we might hook up with a good-looking Army guy or something, but they wouldn't even let us on base. We went all that way just to be told to turn around and go home!"

I stood there sipping my beer, chuckling to myself. What did these girls expect? You can't drive onto a military base and expect the gate guard to wave you right through, no matter how pretty you are.

I admired their spunk, though.

"So we tried to get a room for the night at a local motel, but they were all filled up with everyone who had just returned from the war. We had to sleep in our car! I am not really happy with anything military right now."

I saw one of the girls looking over at me, noticing my smile as I listened to their tale of woe.

"Is something funny?" she inquired.

Damn, she was good looking.

"No, I was just eavesdropping on your conversation and was thinking that Fort Bragg is a long way to go to get a kiss from a military man."

"Is that so?"

"Yup, I bet you could find one closer to home if you looked hard enough."

"Really? Do you know anyone around here who's in the military?"

"As a matter of fact, I do. I could probably introduce you, if you buy me a beer."

"Okay, you have a deal. I buy you a drink and you introduce me to a military man."

We shook on it and a round of beers soon appeared.

Taking a sip out of my fresh bottle, I stuck my hand out and introduced myself, "Hi, my name is John. What's yours?"

"Lisa, and this is my friend, Kim. Now, John, where's the military guy you promised me?"

"I'm right here."

"What? You mean you? You're not in the military! You're just saying that because you heard us talking."

"Hell, we just met and already you're calling me a liar. Tell you what, if I can prove that I'm in the Navy, will you buy me another beer?"

"Okay, but there's no way you're in the service!"

Smiling, I pulled my military identification card out of my wallet, and handed it over to her for closer inspection.

"Petty Officer First Class John Quinn, United States Navy, at your service, ma'am."

"Well, I'll be damned! Hello, sailor."

And that's how I met Lisa.

Because of the physical effects and limitations caused by cerebral palsy, I've always been awkward and shy around women. Being tall, thin, and walking like the tin man did nothing for my confidence and I always felt like that skinny kid who never won a match on the wrestling mat. With Lisa, I felt different. The words came easy and we hit it off right from the start.

At dinner the following day we talked for hours. It was as if I had known her all my life. I told her what it was like to live on board a ship and travel the world.

"So you've been to the Eiffel Tower?"

"Sure have …ate dinner there one night."

"And saw the pyramids in Egypt?"

"Yup. I actually climbed inside."

"That's just incredible! I don't think that I'll ever see those sights, John. I bet you have a girl in every port. Am I right?"

"Nope. I'm not much of a ladies' man, Lisa."

"Well, you could have fooled me there, sailor."

She was impressed, and I wanted her to be. This girl was special and I knew it.

We left the restaurant and I escorted her to her car, wondering if I should kiss her. I wanted to in the worst way, but still felt uncertain if she shared those feelings.

"Lisa, I can't believe that I just met you yesterday and have to head back to my ship tomorrow. Why couldn't I have met you two weeks ago when my vacation began?"

"John, I know what you mean. I feel terrible that you have to leave in the morning. I want you to stay here so that we can get to know each other better. But I do have one more question for you."

"Sure. What is that?"

"I've always wondered what it's like to kiss a military man. Are you going to just stand there or am I going to find out?"

"I think I can help you out there, ma'am," I said, laughing.

We kissed and I suddenly felt like anything was possible, anything.

The following morning, I called Lisa before I headed out to the airport.

"I didn't sleep a wink last night."

"I understand, John. I kept thinking about the wonderful time I had with you yesterday."

"To hell with that. I was thinking about our kiss!"

It was tough to get on that airplane, but Lisa and I promised to communicate when we could. It was a promise I intended to keep.

As soon as I returned to the *USS Chandler*, I called her. Then I sat down and wrote her a letter and waited with great anticipation for that first mail call to see if Lisa would write me back as promised. She did. Within a week, I had six letters tucked under the bunk of my mattress, each smelling sweeter than the one before.

Before long, I was calling and writing every day. With each announcement of mail call, I'd receive another letter or card from Lisa. The guys in my office said that I was getting the most mail on the entire ship.

However, even as our relationship progressed, and each letter unfolded a bit more of our lives to one another, I still didn't have the courage to tell her about my cerebral palsy. I thought it might scare her away, so like with the Navy, I kept that secret to myself. She must have noticed something, but she never said a word.

Time passed quickly, and the *Chandler* was eventually ordered back to the Persian Gulf for a six-month deployment.

Before the ship departed, I was granted a week's leave and flew home to be with Lisa. I didn't tell my family or even Phil about the trip. I wanted to spend as much time with her as possible.

It was hell tearing myself away from her arms after a week of pure joy, but it was time to do my duty and head into a war zone. While on deployment, I contacted Lisa at every opportunity. I called from Hawaii, Japan, Hong Kong, and Bahrain. The cards and letters continued and soon my locker was filled to capacity. I read and re-read each one before going to sleep at night. She said she couldn't wait to introduce her military man to friends and family, and hoped we could be together soon.

When the ship returned from six long months at sea, Lisa was there on the San Diego pier, holding up a sign on a long pole that could be seen from a mile away.

"Welcome Home, Big John," it read. It made me feel like the luckiest sailor in California!

We spent a special week together in Coronado, walking the beach, touring the Hotel Del Coronado, and enjoying each other's company. It was the best time of my life. Stopping for lunch at McPs, a local SEAL hangout, our talk turned toward the future.

I had been in the Navy for nine years and was getting ready to negotiate orders to shore duty. One of the misconceptions that people have about the Navy is that a sailor spends all his time on a ship, out to sea. This is not true. Each job has its own sea/shore rotation. After spending so much time on board ship, the Navy would then send or "rotate" the sailor in military slang, to shore duty. My rotation was three years at sea, followed by three years of shore duty. Shore duty is great because you are basically working 8 a.m. until 4 p.m. You drive to work, can purchase a house, and start a family, which is just what I had in mind.

I had recently taken the advancement examination for chief petty officer. I expected the results to be published within a few days and felt confident that I would be promoted. It was just a matter of waiting for the results. Interestingly, Lisa seemed more excited than I at the thought of my earning such a prestigious promotion at such a young age.

"John, let's talk about your next assignment. Do you think it's possible to get orders to Michigan after you make chief?" she asked over a large bowl of French onion soup.

I had been anticipating this question for some time and had given it some serious thought. I knew she wanted a more normal life as a couple.

"Well, I'm planning to call the detailer next week and see what's available. Maybe I can get recruiting duty in the Detroit area someplace. Would you like that?"

"Oh, John, that would be great!"

"I'll contact them first thing Monday."

I called, and the Navy laughed.

The closest transfer I could get to my hometown was Great Lakes, Illinois, where I had gone to boot camp. Try as I might, the detailer did not budge on my Michigan idea. When I informed

Lisa about this development, she was very unhappy and slammed the phone on the receiver. She refused to pick up when I tried to call her back.

Things got worse the following day with the announcement that I did not get selected for advancement to chief petty officer. I was sure I was going to be chosen. I took it personally. How could the Navy do this to me? It would be another long year before I could take the test again. Damn Navy!

I needed a shoulder to lean on and called Lisa. She wasn't there to comfort me. I left the bad news on her answering machine.

The phone calls from Lisa stopped. I tried to reach her a dozen times, with the same result. She would not accept my calls.

And I received one more letter. It began: "Dear John."

I was heartsick *and* angry. I blamed the Navy. How could they do this to me! My future was ruined.

I moped around the ship for a couple of days, unable to concentrate on anything until an item crossed my desk that seemed like an answer to my prayers. The Navy was offering money to sailors to *leave* the service.

Quickly reading the directive, I realized that I was eligible to receive a lump sum payment of $30,000 to get out of the Navy. I would be able to return to Michigan, start a civilian career and a whole new life with Lisa by my side.

I submitted my request to leave the Navy.

Within 24 hours, I was called into the CO's office. He was not a happy man.

"Yeoman Quinn, what the hell is going on with you?" he barked, holding my chit in his hand.

"I want to get out of the Navy, sir, and go back home to Michigan."

"What the hell for? Is this about that girl you introduced to me a few weeks ago?"

"Yes, sir."

"Word has it that you received a 'Dear John' letter."

On a relatively small ship like a destroyer, it was hard to keep a secret.

"Yes, sir. That's true."

"So, you think leaving the Navy and starting a life with this woman is the right decision for you?"

"Yes, sir."

The captain stared at me then shook his head in disgust.

"Petty Officer Quinn, you have your head so far up your ass, you don't know which way is up. You're one of the finest sailors I've ever met and you want to throw your entire career away over some woman? Son, I thought you were smarter than that!"

I stood there silent. What could I say? I loved Lisa.

"Let me tell you another thing. If you do this, you'll live to regret it. Sure, the Navy is going to give you a few bucks to leave, but after taxes, you won't be left with much. How many years do you have in, right now?"

"Just over nine, sir."

"You didn't make chief this time. Am I right?"

"That's correct, sir."

"I am surprised you didn't make it, but after all, it was only your first time up. I can almost guarantee that you'll make it next year. Becoming a chief at the ten year mark is something special, son. Hell, if you wanted to, you could become an officer. Do you realize that?"

"Yes, sir."

"And knowing all this, you still want me to endorse your decision?"

"Yes, sir."

"You are a fool."

I stood silent. I just wanted out.

"Tell you what I am going to do, Quinn. I'm going to do you a favor. I want you to take a week off. Go fly home to this girl and talk over your future with her. If you come back to the ship and still feel strongly about getting out of the Navy, I'll sign your request and you will be on your way. But if you come back and want to change your mind, I will tear up this paperwork and we'll never speak of it again. Deal?"

The captain stuck his hand out and I shook it.

"You have a deal, Captain."

I was on the next plane home. After a long flight to Detroit Metropolitan Airport, I hopped into a taxi and went straight to Lisa's house. She would be happy at my news! We would laugh, hug, and celebrate our future together.

I was wrong.

When she opened her front door and saw me, she slammed the door in my face. I actually heard the deadbolt lock slide into place.

I was left standing on her porch, stunned.

What the hell just happened?

What do I do now? My mind was spinning. Looking to the street, I saw the taxi driver, glancing up from behind the wheel of his yellow cab, watching the scene unfold. I could see that he had kept the engine running. Smart guy.

I walked in a daze back to the cab.

I never saw Lisa again.

I did rotate to shore duty, but instead of winding up in Michigan with Lisa, I was offered and quickly accepted an assignment back across the bridge in Coronado, California, working again with my SEAL friends at Naval Special Warfare Group ONE.

It was a mistake. Coronado held too many memories of my time together with Lisa. I couldn't walk into a restaurant or run past the Hotel Del without thinking of her and what a loser I was. Shore duty also afforded me more free time than the constant demands of life at sea. I often went to one of the local bars after work and that's where I was on Christmas Eve, 1993. I was lonely, sad, angry, and very, very drunk.

"You alright to drive there, John?" inquired Anthony from behind the counter.

By this time, I was on a first name basis with many of the bartenders and waitresses in the area.

"Do you want me to call you a taxi?"

As always, I answered, "No, I'll be okay."

Another mistake.

The Coronado police picked me up and arrested me a few minutes later as I drove erratically down Orange Avenue towards the naval base where I lived. I lost my driving privileges for 90 days, paid a fine, and had to pick up trash on the side of the road for a few months.

My command, shocked at the arrest of such a fine sailor, decided that my DUI was an isolated incident and allowed the civilian court to deal with me. I swore never to drink again and I kept my word. But only for those ninety days.

Mom, in recovery herself and doing great, sent me a large package of twelve-step material which I glanced at briefly, but quickly threw away. Mom needed to get sober, not me. I just needed to control my drinking better. That was the key.

When the 90 days were up, car keys in hand, I headed out to the nearest pub to make up for lost time.

In my dress whites

10

Life on a Carrier

My time on board the *Iowa* proved to be every bit as challenging as I imagined. But without question the most physically demanding ships I called home were Nimitz-class aircraft carriers. I was stationed on board two; *USS Dwight D. Eisenhower* and *USS John C. Stennis.* Carriers in this class are almost 1200 feet long and 300 feet wide. They have 16 floors, close to 3,000 rooms, and, with an embarked air wing, a crew of 5,000 people. The flight deck, where aircraft fly on and off, is more than four acres in size! The carrier is a 97,000 ton floating city that can be summoned out to sea at a moment's notice and be gone for years. To be up close to a carrier is to feel its power. To serve on one is to know its size. And there's only one way to get around a ship. You walk.

As a young boy, my mom was always reminding me to walk properly. I can still hear her voice in my head as I sit here and type the words.

"John, get off your tiptoes! Walk heel and toe!"

Most people normally don't give walking a second thought. They just walk. No big deal. Not for me. I have to concentrate on every single step I take. Every single step.

On the carrier there are no elevators or escalators. Climbing stairs became a huge daily trial. As the senior yeoman, I was in charge of the captain's administrative office, located on the 03 level or third floor above the main deck. Out at sea, the commanding officer relocated his office to the bridge on the 09 level, where his presence ensured the safe steerage of the ship. The captain also monitors the ship's airplanes taking off and landing. The CO, (captain or skipper), of an aircraft carrier never leaves the bridge during flight operations, and that's the primary duty of an aircraft carrier—flying military aircraft, sometimes 24 hours a day.

In my capacity as the administrative assistant to the CO, I went to where he was located, and had to climb six very steep flights of stairs, up and down, all day long. On average, I made that trek 30 times a day to deliver phone messages, empty the CO's correspondence in-box, or answer any question that he might have concerning his daily schedule. Whenever the captain called, I had to be up on the bridge as quickly as possible. Heel toe. Heel toe.

If I were on the main deck of the ship—which meant nine flights of stairs—I had to grab the railings to keep from falling, a maneuver made even more difficult with my arms loaded down with correspondence for the captain's signature. And keep in mind that a ship moves as it churns through the water, making it a very unstable platform. Because of the cerebral palsy, with its miscommunication between brain and body, my balance and depth perception have always been poor. Stairs were my nemesis.

One of the tricks that I learned to keep from falling was to lean way back as I navigated down the steep stairs. This kept my center of balance back on my heels, helped steady my tall frame, and kept me from falling when the ship was pitching and rolling in high seas. I also did occasionally revert to my childhood method of pulling myself up using the railing, but only when I knew no one could see me.

To make getting around the ship even more interesting, vessels at sea set a condition at sunset called darken ship. Darken ship makes the passageways glow blood red in an eerie, haunted-house sort of way. This ensures that the officer of the deck maintains his night vision, an important issue for safe navigation. If even one "white" light shone on the water, it would take valuable minutes for the bridge team to regain night vision. Imagine you are out on your back patio stargazing at night. And just as you spot the Orion nebula, your neighbor's porch light blinks on for a few seconds. It was like that.

Going up the stairs to the bridge to converse with the captain was always an adventure when the lights were bright, but during darken ship, I had to climb stairs basically in the dark, often in rough seas that made the ship pitch back and forth as well as side to side.

Most of the young sailors I worked with bounced around the ship with ease, having little or no difficulty with either the stairs or the walking distances. I lived with unrelenting pain from my deformities. Cerebral palsy affects a child's growing muscles and bones. As an adult, this uneven development of my leg, knees, and hips, as well as the resulting misalignment of spine and shoulders, made getting around the ship extremely difficult. Imagine the tin man again, only now he is half-rusted. His feet are also probably flat like mine.

The shoes didn't help. It wasn't like I could wear comfortable running shoes as I climbed mile after mile during my time at sea. Steel-toed boots are a mandatory safety requirement for the crew on board a Navy ship. It took forever to break them in and they were a lot heavier on my feet. By the end of the day, my muscles were so fatigued, I could barely lift my trembling, exhausted legs.

When I become tired, I have a tendency to drag my feet along behind me. This symptom is common to cerebral palsy sufferers. I get angry when I catch myself not picking my feet up and walking properly. Of course, during my years at sea, I was also always afraid the ship's doctor would pull me aside and ask me what the problem was with my legs. After a long day of climbing and walking for miles in my steel-toed shoes, I really had to focus on lifting each foot up and placing it down, willing my body forward in a natural, smooth motion. I remained on constant guard against limping or dragging my feet and thus betraying my secret. My psyche was as exhausted as my body.

Standing watch on board a Navy ship while in port was another form of torture. The Navy takes the 24 hour days and breaks them into six four-hour watches. This team of watchstanders, pulled from all hands, is called the in-port duty section, whose primary responsibility is guarding against any threat: intruders, fire, flood, or medical emergency, day and night.

"Standing" the watch literally means standing for four full hours. Sometimes, due to a shortage of qualified personnel, we stand two watches, or eight hours of being on our feet: no sitting down in a chair, no going to take a break. We stand a vigilant watch, and this duty is taken very seriously. Most of the time, because I worked for the captain and was extremely busy during daylight hours, I stood my watches after the skipper departed the ship.

On my assigned duty day, I would work 12 hours and also stand a four-hour watch at night, normally midnight to four in the morning, then be back in my office by seven to greet the captain. I did this every four days when the ship was in port. To illustrate how difficult this was, imagine standing with one heel raised an inch higher than the other. That position throws off the hips, shoulders and spine, and quickly moves beyond the realm of mere discomfort. By the end of my four-hour watch, my back and hips would be numb with pain, my shoulders aching, and my flat feet fast asleep.

It's a source of pride for me knowing that I *never* missed a watch: when it was my turn to stand duty, I did so with honor.

Even when not standing watch, the actual workday was very long and exhausting, especially for the senior yeoman on a warship. Regardless of whether the ship was at sea or in port, my alarm clock would jolt me awake at 4:30 a.m. I needed to be in my office well before the captain's arrival at seven to ensure that his schedule for the day was still current, his correspondence in-box prioritized with the hottest items placed on top, and the previous night's message traffic sorted and highlighted. Reveille would sound throughout the entire ship at six with the officer of the deck striking four bells.

"Reveille, reveille! All hands heave out and trice up!" Followed quickly by, "Breakfast for the crew."

Oftentimes, the next announcement would be: "Petty Officer Quinn, please contact the executive officer in his inport cabin." Hearing this brought a sense of dread because it meant that there was some sort of administrative problem requiring immediate attention. More often than not, something *was* wrong, the end result being that I got my butt chewed by the ship's second in command while everyone else was still rubbing the sleep from their eyes. It was a great way to start the day.

If I wasn't summoned up to the XO's stateroom, I would head to breakfast. The entire crew knew that I worked in the captain's office, with direct access to the old man, so my ham and cheese omelet usually came with questions or pleas for help...

"Hey, John, I hear that the ship is pulling into Bahrain a day early. Is it true?"

"Quinn, did the captain review that instruction last night? I really need to make sure he signs it today."

"Chief, I need to get on the CO's schedule for ten minutes today. Can you find me a slot and fit me in?"

Everybody wanted something and I was the guy who could deliver. Never mind the fact that I was enjoying my morning cup of coffee and would soon be up in my office until well into the night... if someone had an administrative problem, saw me and asked for my help, I'd do what I could. Everyone knew that. Heck, one time I was in the shower and somebody tracked me down to see if I'd get the captain to sign something.

By 6:30 a.m. or so, once I had climbed the stairs and entered the office, it would be controlled madness for the rest of the long day. Phones ringing, officers with pay concerns, new arrivals to the ship with paperwork to process, the captain with questions about his schedule. When you worked in the administrative office of a battleship or an aircraft carrier, the pressure to perform was intense and, for me, this constant emotional stress also took a toll on my body. I'd stagger down to my bunk, long after everyone had retired for the night, with a pounding headache, eyes blurry from staring at a computer screen all day, and a body tortured with pain.

At my desk on the carrier

Getting rest on board a ship wasn't like going to sleep at home—no king size beds here! Racks are stacked three high, with the bed above you inches from your nose as you lay on your back. You can't roll over and get comfortable without hitting your shoulder on the bed above you. Mattresses measure an inch and a half thick and lay atop a steel plate that measures six feet by three feet. I am six feet, four inches—longer than my bed. For many years, I was unable to properly stretch out and fully relax my back or hips after a long day at work.

My muscles and joints cried out for relief, and crying is exactly what I wanted to do when painful leg cramps would come at night. I'd have flashbacks to childhood as I screamed into my pillow. This time my yelling would have woken up an entire aircraft carrier, not just my brothers. The cramps in my calves were so debilitating that I was kept awake many nights. I dealt with the pain by walking them out, no easy task. Trying to put weight on those cramped legs was excruciating, and difficult to do in our confined sleeping area.

Every time I was home on leave, I'd luxuriate in my own bed, wondering how I could have ever taken it for granted. Sometimes the smell of Mom's laundry detergent alone made me wish I could stay there forever.

My height also made life on board ship tough in other ways. The passageways are lined with piping for jet fuel, loops are built into the ceiling to store firefighting water, and there are thousands of miles of electrical cables, all which severely reduces ceiling clearance for tall guys like me. I was constantly ducking my head to avoid hitting these obstacles as I made my way around the ship. In fact, I couldn't stand up straight while I walked down a passageway. If I did, I would have smacked my head! I was always moving with a bent over stride, my hunched back hurting more every passing day. I'm sure it appeared rather odd too, much like the Hunchback of Notre Dame on his way to the bell tower.

You know what else looked comical? It was my limbs, which still can suddenly and without notice shake and shudder vigorously. The medical term is "muscle spasticity," a common cerebral palsy symptom. I'm okay when I talk or move around, but standing in one spot knowing that everyone is looking at me can be the trigger that starts me trembling like a man walking towards the electric chair.

I remember a time I had to get up in front of my fellow sailors while stationed on board the *Eisenhower*. As a senior chief yeoman, one of my many jobs was to prepare commendations for deserving sailors. The captain of the ship would sign these military decorations, and the medals would be presented in a formal ceremony in front of the awardees' entire department. With over 5,000 personnel in 13 departments on board the ship, it took a lot to organize these award ceremonies, but I loved seeing my shipmates get recognized for their hard work and dedication.

As much as I enjoyed preparing these awards for presentation, there was one thing I did not look forward to—getting an award myself. I was honored to receive every Navy decoration that I earned, but receiving a medal meant that I had to stand in front of everyone, giving my body every opportunity to tremble and spasm, exposing me to ridicule and potentially uncovering my secret.

When my boss, the administrative officer, told me I was receiving the Navy commendation medal for work completed during a six-month Arabian Gulf deployment, I was indeed humbled, but at the same time terrified.

That night, down in the ship's print shop, I was called up to stand in front of the entire administrative department.

"Senior Chief Quinn, front and center."

Lord, please help keep my body under control.

"The Secretary of the Navy takes great pleasure…" As the narrator began to read my citation, the twitching began in my foot, moving quickly up the leg. I tried to concentrate, to keep the tremors from spreading, but it was no use. I could hear the sailors in ranks behind me, snickering and laughing.

By the time my awards presentation concluded, I was trembling all over and totally embarrassed. The skipper came up after the ceremony and asked if I was all right.

Oh sure, now that the comedy show was over.

11

Hitting Bottom

Because of cerebral palsy, I have always been quiet and shy. I only felt at ease socially when I was drinking in bars in local ports with the guys. Beer was everywhere and I was good at drinking it. It helped me become an accepted member within the fraternity of Navy beer drinkers and give me the sense of belonging that I craved.

Every occasion seemed to call for a drink...

"Hey, Quinn, we're all getting together at Mario's when the ship pulls in tomorrow. Are you coming with us?"

"John, congratulations on your promotion! The first round is on me!"

"Thanks for typing up that award for me today, John. Let me get you a beer."

You bet.

It seemed the more often I drank, the bigger my circle of acquaintances grew. For a guy who didn't have many friends as a kid, this new camaraderie felt great. I would walk into a bar on a Friday night and run into a couple of sailors from my ship. After a few drinks, we were lifelong buddies.

I could always justify a bottle of beer in my mind. Bad day? Hey, don't worry. Toss back a couple of drinks and make your troubles go away. Good day? Great! Let's go celebrate.

Besides, I worked hard and earned the right to sit and have a beer or two. On board ship, everyone wanted a piece of my time, from the moment I awoke until the captain departed the ship for the day. The bar was the one place I was not asked about getting a signature on an award or instruction, nor was the administrative officer breathing down my back about the cleanliness of the passageway. I began to look forward, with great anticipation, to happy hour and a moment of peace.

When I was out to sea, I never drank. It wasn't formally served on board except in the rare instance that a warship was out for more than 90 days consecutively. In that event, every crewmember got two beers. When the ship finally pulled into port, I went to the nearest bar. It was making up for lost time.

I rationalized when I realized I was drinking heavily: who was I hurting? I wasn't missing work. I was getting promoted at a rapid pace with glowing personnel evaluations. I was single, didn't have children and paid my bills on time. If I wanted to drink, that was my business. Besides, everyone else in my circle was guzzling just as much as I was. What's the harm in that?

Drinking seemed to ease my social awkwardness, emotional issues and work stress. Alcohol may have also helped alleviate my physical pain, although I was not conscious of this as a motivating factor. I mostly drank to fit in and escape. It felt good… for a while.

On one fateful morning, I sat on my sofa with my head in my hands trying to recount events of the night before. My hands were shaking and my wallet was empty. I vaguely remembered my car being towed, the police car with the red flickering lights, the cell.

Oh Lord, the arrest.

I'd only gone out for a few beers. What the hell happened?

I was at a crossroad. I could either continue down the path I was on, trying to control my drinking, or I could try something different and get some help.

I made two phone calls, the first to my commanding officer, who after listening patiently to my situation told me that we would sit down and talk about my problem at length first thing

Monday morning. His support and understanding meant a great deal to me at that point in my naval career.

The second call was to my mom.

"Mom, I think I have a drinking problem."

"Welcome to the club, son."

I was finally ready to listen, even desperate for her advice.

"Just don't drink for the rest of the day, John. Try to get some sleep. Sounds like you've had a long night."

I dozed off and was awakened by a knock on my apartment door. Startled by the sound, I dragged my body out of bed and cracked open the door, not wanting to admit the killer California sunlight. My sister Susan stared back at me. I was speechless. What was she doing here? Doesn't she live in Arizona? My mind was in a fog.

"Mom told me about your phone call and we are worried about you. So I figured I'd fly over and see how you're getting along."

"I'm not doing too well, Suz."

My eyes struggled to stay open and I led Susan into my little apartment, staggering in the process.

"Yes, I can see that. Let's see about getting you some help. Where's your phone book?"

The following day I was sitting in a 12 step meeting for alcoholics.

It was in an alley just a few blocks from my apartment. I had walked past the place a thousand times and never knew it was there. I went wearily to a non-descript entry way. Two women sat nearby on a worn wooden bench and sipped coffee in the warm sunshine.

"Looks like you could use a meeting."

"I guess so. Do I walk right in?"

"Yup, we've been waiting for you. The meeting will start in a couple of minutes."

What did she just say? They've been waiting for me? How did she know I was coming?

I quickly walked in before someone else saw me and strategically chose a chair between the exit and a small bathroom. I could either run quickly out the door if I freaked or hopefully make it into the bathroom if I needed to puke, and I felt like doing both. Adjusting my eyes to the dimly lit space, I could make out worn couches, mismatched chairs and a beat-up coffee table. About a dozen people sat comfortably talking among themselves. Everyone seemed to know each other. There was a relaxed feeling about the place. A silver-haired man came over and introduced himself.

"Hi, I'm Tom, what's your name?"

"John." *What the hell does this guy want? Is he going to try and save my soul?*

"Is this your first time at a meeting, John?"

"Yes. Do I have to sign in or anything? Do I have to pay money to come in here?"

I had no idea what to expect. Tom just smiled at me and said, "No, just sit back and listen to the people as they talk. See if you can identify with what's being said, okay?"

"Okay, thanks."

"You look like you could use a cup of coffee, John. Want me to get you some? It's free."

"A cup of coffee would be wonderful right now."

I felt like crying. What the hell was I was doing in such a place? I felt I didn't belong with these people. I had stature, responsibility, and wore a uniform. Believing this may have been a total mistake, I almost got up to leave, but was trapped by some guy named Tom. He handed me a half cup of coffee in a white Styrofoam cup, plopped down next to me and the meeting began.

The facilitator of the meeting asked if there was anyone in the room who was present for their first meeting and would like to introduce themselves. I slowly raised my hand and all eyes turned in my direction. "This is my first meeting. My name is John."

"Hi, John!" Everyone said loudly in unison.

I must have jumped several feet out of my chair, hot coffee splashed all over my lap. People laughed and smiled at me. I looked over to the door and wanted to bolt. Sensing this, Tom put his hand on my shoulder, "Relax, John, just keep an open mind and listen."

I did and was stunned by what I heard. It seemed that these people knew exactly how I drank! How did they know? I thought I was the only one who drank like I did. It was as if they were right inside my head, reading my thoughts. Leaning in intently, I learned that alcoholics cannot control the amount of alcohol they drink, once they start. They have a physical allergy coupled with a mental obsession that makes it almost impossible to stop drinking. It just takes one beer. It wasn't the fact that I drank so much, it was the fact that I drank at all. I was stunned by this vital piece of information.

This simple truth helped explain so much. I could never understand why I couldn't control my drinking. I would walk into a bar at five o'clock in the evening and tell myself that I would only have a couple of beers.

And I meant it. I usually had to get up early for work, or had an important meeting early in the day. My intention was to have a couple of beers to relax and then head straight home. But then I would look at my watch and see that it was suddenly 11 p.m. Where did the time go? I learned that it was the first round of beers that got me drunk, not the last one. Total abstinence from alcohol seemed to be the only answer.

My idea of an alcoholic was a smelly person who pushed his worldly belongings down Main Street in a shopping cart, slept under a bridge or in a homeless shelter. He drank cheap wine out of a paper sack and panhandled money. I wasn't one of those people. I drank Guinness Stout.

Looking around the room, I saw people just like me. I discovered that there were doctors, businessmen, and lawyers, many in nice suits, ties, and dresses in the crowd. Not a disgusting one in the bunch. If anything, I was the one out of place, with my bloodshot eyes, shaking hands, and empty wallet. I noticed their eyes. They sparkled with a joy for life, an ease of living that I didn't have. I wondered how you got that.

I told the group my story, how I was arrested for Driving Under the Influence (DUI) just down the block, the second DUI arrest I had gotten in the past five years. I was sure the Navy would kick me out. I was terrified that I faced the possibility of going to civilian prison for at least six months. I told the group that I thought my life was over.

They laughed. Right out loud. At me.

What the hell? Here I am, telling these strangers the torment I'd been through the past 24 hours and they respond by laughing at me.

I turned to Tom and asked, "Why do they laugh?"

"They are not laughing at you, they're laughing with you. We have all been where you are now. Only someone who has been in your desperate situation, and recovered, can laugh at it. In time, you'll understand."

I would come to learn that all those folks have sat in the same chair I had occupied. They understood my pain. I thought of my mother and father, who in the past had both drank to excess with sometimes serious consequences. I learned that not everyone who drinks is an alcoholic, but I could now see the pattern a bit clearer. Mom had been trying to tell me for years she was an alcoholic, but I refused to listen. Denying her issues helped me deny my own.

When the hour-long meeting was concluded, many people came up to me and gave me words of encouragement.

"I am glad you came today, John. Keep coming back, okay?"

"Here's my phone number. If you feel like taking a drink, give me a call and let's talk about it."

"Sounds like you have hit your bottom, kid. It never has to be this bad ever again." Wow. These people seemed to care about me. One gentleman came up to me and said he had been sober for 23 years. He looked me square in the eye and said, "There is hope for you."

I turned to Tom as I was walking out the door.

"Tom, does this mean that I can never have a beer again?"

He stopped and smiled. "Sure, you can take a drink, John. Nobody is telling you any different. But let me ask you a question. Do you think drinking has made your life unmanageable?"

All I could do was nod my aching head in slow agreement.

"Remember this—you can't get drunk if you don't take that first drink."

I obviously would be welcomed back to another 12-step meeting tomorrow.

But what about the United States Navy? Would they want me back after learning the full details of my arrest? It's not everyday that a senior chief gets locked up. I knew my bosses would be upset and I was right. I sat silently at headquarters early the next morning in a closed door meeting with the CO and XO, the commanding and executive officers. The incident report of my arrest was on the desk, providing a full account of my stupidity. There was nothing I could say as the barrage of comments rained down.

"What the hell happened, Senior? Damn it! I thought you had better sense than this!"

"Do you realize how embarrassing this makes the command look?"

"Why didn't you just call a cab if you had so much to drink?"

Then the XO, the executive officer, asked me a simple question. "This *is* your first offense, right?"

I stared down at my feet and said one word. "No."

This new revelation left the CO and XO speechless. Their mouths hung open with the shocking news that one of their most trusted enlisted leaders was now a repeat DUI offender.

The Commanding Officer was looking quickly through my official service record. "I don't see anything in here about that."

"You won't find anything in there, sir. My command determined it was a civil matter. Nothing was ever entered into my file."

The skipper looked at me with a newfound disgust. "That's an incredible mistake on their part, but very lucky for you. You know that we have the authority to send you home on just this one arrest, don't you?"

"Yes, sir, I realize that." It was true and it's what I expected to happen. As a senior chief petty officer I would go to courts-martial and be discharged from the Navy with a Bad Conduct

Discharge (BCD). My nightmare scenario about being kicked out of the Navy was about to come true, but it had nothing to do with my cerebral palsy.

The CO stopped his line of attack and just looked out the window for a bit. I could tell he was thinking hard. Finally, he turned to me.

"Did you go to treatment after your first arrest? Receive any type of counseling at all?"

"No, sir. Nothing was offered to me." It was true. I was never ordered to rehab, mandated to attend 12-step meetings, or even advised to seek help through my command drug and alcohol counselor. I tried to quit drinking on my own after my first arrest.

"Would you go now if it was offered to you?"

"Yes, sir, I would." I meant that with all my heart.

"Good, because here's the deal, Senior. I believe you have a drinking problem and are very sick. If you get the help you need, I believe you have the potential to continue your career. Now, I'll have to get approval for this. That will be tough sell, but I think the Admiral will okay it. If you successfully complete treatment and the prescribed follow-on care, I'll recommend that you be retained in the Navy. But I also promise you this. If I so much as smell booze on you, see you in the supermarket with beer in your shopping cart, or a little birdie lands on my shoulder and whispers in my ear that you are drinking in town, I will kick you out of my Navy so fast it will make your head spin. Hell, I'll type the paperwork up myself. And as far as the civilian courts go, you are on your own. I suggest you get yourself a good lawyer."

Now it was my turn to be speechless. I was going to get the help I desperately wanted and needed. It was the start of my long journey out of the darkness.

I have been sober ever since.

The civilian court system and the Department of Motor Vehicles were not so kind. They didn't care about my military background, rank, or the number of ribbons on my chest. Only one thing mattered—guilt or innocence. I took the skipper's advice and got a lawyer. We sat down in his office a few days before my court appearance to go over my situation.

"From what I see here, this is your second offense in the past five years, is that correct?"

"Yes, sir it is."

"I also have the results of your blood test. Your Blood Alcohol Content (BAC) is extremely high. I'm going to be honest; the court will not look favorably on that, especially for someone who is a repeat offender. Are you prepared to go to jail for 90 days, John? Because that's exactly what you're looking at here."

"Yes, sir, I am."

Being a naval administrator, I knew that if I went to jail for anything over 30 days, I would be automatically placed in an Unauthorized Absence (UA) status and immediately discharged. If my jail sentence was less than 30 days, I could use my vacation time and it would be authorized. A 90 day jail sentence would end my military career. But I couldn't change the past, only deal with the present, no matter how grim it all looked. "One day at a time" was a recently-learned slogan I was trying hard to adopt.

"I see here that you are now enrolled in treatment. Is this through the Navy?"

"Yes, it is. I am also attending 12-step meetings as well."

"Okay, that's all well and good, but the best thing I think we can do is plead guilty and hope for the best."

After heated deliberation, with my career and maybe my life in the balance, the lawyer worked a plea bargain that kept me out of prison. A partial list of my sentence included the loss of my driver's license for 18 months, fines and penalties totaling more than $10,000, and two months of working on the weekends picking up trash, cleaning toilets, sweeping parking lots, and whatever else the city of San Diego decided was best for me that day.

It may look like I paid a heavy price for my last night of drinking, but in reality I got off easy and I know it. I didn't go to jail, completed my treatment, and got retained in the Navy. I had to walk to work, take the bus everywhere for a couple of years, and picked up trash in the California rain for a couple of months. I also lost something that was very important to me—the respect of my young sailors. But it was a very small price to pay for what I did. I could have killed someone that night. I am a very fortunate man.

✧ ✧ ✧

To say that my mom followed my Navy progress closely is an understatement. She *lived* my career, waiting eagerly to hear the latest scoop from her sailor son. Whenever there was a crisis in the world, my mother would be on the phone, wanting answers from me.

"John, CNN says the explosion on board the *Iowa* was caused by one of its sailors. What's the real story?"

"I heard your boss talking today on the news. He seems like a real nice guy. Have you met him yet?"

"Oh, I just heard that your ship, the *Dwight D. Eisenhower*, is the first combatant ship to have women on it. They don't share the bathroom, do they?"

One of the questions I couldn't answer was where the Navy was sending me next and how long I'd be gone. Much of the work I performed in the service was classified and this little fact drove my mom nuts. So one day, she said, "Let's come up with a code, a signal."

"What for, Mom? Why do we need a signal?"

"If you're getting ready to go some place, just tell me 'the eagle has landed.'"

I burst out laughing, but she was serious.

"The eagle has landed, Mom?" I asked after composing myself.

"Sure! You don't have to tell me where you're headed, but if you say that during our conversation, I'll know you're on the move. It'll be our little secret, something just between me and my military boy."

"You got it, Mom. Anything for you."

She obviously watched way too many spy movies.

The television at Mom's house was tuned into CNN 24 hours a day, seven days a week. She watched just in case something happened. In my travels around the globe, I'd send postcards, which she promptly pinned to her bedroom wall. For Christmas, I bought her a sweatshirt that said, "My son is in the U.S. Navy." I think she wore it every day. She was so very proud.

Being the dutiful son, whenever I prepared to deploy to the western Pacific or fly to some exotic sounding locale like Egypt or Paris, I would call my mother and tell her the eagle was landing. Mom would get all serious and say, "I understand, son." It made her happy and I loved it.

Mom was there for me all along. She was in the stands, waving madly as I graduated from boot camp. When the Navy decided to retire the *Iowa*, Mom was in attendance, sitting next to some congressman and feeling right at home. She proudly witnessed my promotion to the rank of chief petty officer, making the trip to Coronado, California, to pin on my anchors.

My mother had such a hard time after Dad's sudden passing. She had coped with her grief by using a potent cocktail of prescription pills downed with liquor. It had taken her years to overcome those issues. To have Mom with me—sober, proud, and happy—as I became Chief Quinn, was such a gift. It made the moment even more special and emotional when I thought of how I almost lost her.

During the fall of 1998 I was stationed on shore duty in Coronado, California. I was just getting home from work when the phone rang. It was Mom.

"Hi, Ma. How's everything going?"

"Pretty good, son. Did you work hard for the Navy today?" She sounded cheerful and upbeat.

"Yes, ma'am," I said chuckling.

"John, there's a reason why I'm calling you. I am sitting here in the doctor's office and just got a bit of news that I need to share."

"Sure, Mom. What is it?"

"The doctor tells me that I have cancer."

"What?"

"I have cancer, John."

"Okay, Mom... how are they going to treat it?"

I was stunned by this news, but figured that if she was there with the doc, they must be discussing treatment options and wanted to inform me on the best course of action to battle the cancer.

"John, don't be angry."

"Why would I be angry with you, Mom?"

"They are giving me six weeks to live."

A silent thunderclap echoed through my head.

"Are you going to be okay, John?"

No, I was not. That moment was the closest I have come to taking a drink in what has become 11 years of sobriety. I clearly remember hanging up the phone, getting out of my chair and walking to the front door, where I placed my hand on the door knob. I had every intention of stepping over to the nearest bar and having a beer when my hand froze in place for several long moments.

I turned around, sat down in my apartment, and cried as memories flooded my mind. I saw visions of surgical tubing, Mom watching silently in the basement as I looped rubber around my skinny legs in a desperate attempt for normalcy.

I thought about the endless hours she sat with me at Children's Hospital physical therapy wing while her other seven children were at home needing her attention and love. If Mom was angry about having to be there with me, she never showed it. She knew that *her* sacrifice would pay off for *me* in the years to come.

My mother was always the person I called when I achieved something special, a milestone such as a promotion or military award. She was often more excited than I was, and that made me feel loved and honored. "I knew you could do it, John," was often the first thing out of her mouth. Always encouraging, she would be the one to pick me up when I was tired, lonely, and afraid.

Mom

"Mom, I can't do this anymore. I'm exhausted," I would often moan through the long-distance wire.

"I know, honey. Just keep going and know that I'm proud of you. Get some rest and things will be better tomorrow."

Six weeks after being diagnosed with cancer, my mom died.

I arrived for my last visit with her the day before she passed away. Mom always liked to see me in uniform and I made the trip from San Diego to her home in Phoenix dressed in my khakis to please her. Under hospice care, she was heavily sedated and unable to speak, drifting in and out of consciousness.

According to my sisters, it was a matter of a few hours.

I entered her bedroom and boomed out a greeting in my deepest military voice, "Hey there, good looking. How the hell are you?"

My hearty tone must have penetrated her subconscious because Mom sat up and looked around, surprising everyone in the room.

Coming quickly to her bedside, I gently placed my hand in hers, leaned over and gave her a kiss. She reached up and brushed the ribbons on my uniform with her hand and smiled.

"The eagle has landed, Mom," I whispered softly in her ear.

Her grin grew wider as she slowly nodded her head in understanding.

12

Walking Out a Winner

"You've had quite a career, Senior Chief. Are you ready to finish it?"

"Yes, sir," I replied to the captain, slowly rising from the comfortable chair in my dress white uniform. The military decorations on my chest chimed like little Christmas bells as I set my coffee cup down.

"Damn, John. You have more medals than I do."

The commanding officer of the aircraft carrier, USS *John C. Stennis* and I had been reflecting back on my twenty years of life in the Navy. In a few moments, we'd walk from his luxurious cabin to perform my last official act as a sailor.

I was retiring as a senior chief petty officer, the second highest enlisted rank in the Navy, a position to which I had risen in just fourteen years. And I did it while having cerebral palsy. I smiled silently to myself, happy in my accomplishment, but relieved that I wouldn't have to keep up the charade any longer.

Tradition and protocol dictated the naval retirement program. After the playing of the national anthem, posting of the colors, and the recitation of the invocation, my chosen guest speaker, the commanding officer, stepped to the podium to say a few words.

As he spoke, my eyes wandered out over the crowd gathered to honor my career. I saw my brothers and sisters who had traveled as far as twenty-four hundred miles to join me, seated proudly in the front row alongside my best friend, Phil.

The command master chief, the senior enlisted man on board the ship, came to the podium and presented me with a marble plaque of the *John C. Stennis*. As I set the beautiful plaque on the presentation table with all the other mementos of the day, the master of ceremonies said, "Ladies and Gentlemen, Senior Chief John Quinn."

It was now my turn to step up to the microphone and say a few words.

Looking out across the aircraft carrier, I thought of that year down in the basement doing duck walks with thick rubber tubing. Tears came so quickly that I could barely see the speech I'd prepared. Adjusting the microphone, I swallowed hard, took a deep breath, said a prayer of thanks, and hoped I wouldn't shake too much as I spoke from the heart...

> Officers and men of the *John C. Stennis*, fellow chief petty officers, family and friends, thank you for being here today and sharing in this special moment with me. It has been said that the longest journey begins with a single step. Well, my journey began in the seventh grade as a strapping 78 pounder on the wrestling team. I joined the team because I wanted to be part of something and maybe, find out something about myself. Problem was, I was not a very good wrestler. My body was just not strong enough.
>
> One day, the coach came up to me and said, "You're cut off the team. Clean out your locker." When the team's best wrestler, Phil Freeman, heard about this, he went to the coach and said, "If he goes, I go." The coach could see that Phil meant what he said, so I got to stay on the team, and in fact, wrestled all the way through high school.
>
> Now, I would love to tell you that I blossomed into an all-state grappler with countless victories

188

Giving my retirement speech

under my belt, but that did not happen. To be honest, I did not win one match. Ever. But I did win a friendship, one that has grown over the past 20 years and continues to this very day. Thanks, Phil.

You know a funny thing happens when you put in your retirement papers. A floodgate opens in your mind and so many memories come rushing back. If you will indulge me, I would like to share a few with you.

My brother Mike coming home from Navy boot camp in 1973 with short hair and dog tags. I was eleven years old then and I thought it all was so cool.

Telling my family of my decision to join the Navy. My older brothers held me down and beat me up while my younger brothers wanted to know if they could now have the big bed.

Having Mom and Dad come to my boot camp graduation and seeing the mixture of pride, disbelief, and happiness on their faces as I walked up to them in my dress blues for the first time. My parents are in my thoughts as I stand here and I miss them very much.

Getting orders to SEAL Team THREE and asking the question, "What kind of a ship is THAT?"

I think about the Marines in Beirut.

And working at U.S. Central Command and being on the phone with U.S. warships as they were attacked by Iranian speedboats.

I remember the *Samuel B. Roberts* and the *Princeton* hitting floating mines during Operation Earnest Will.

Being in the Egyptian desert with my trusty Xerox 860, typing post exercise reports at 0300 with a four-star Marine proofreading over my shoulder as I sweated over the keyboard.

And I remember 19 April 1989 and the 47 who perished. The crew of the *Iowa* was the finest group of sailors I have ever sailed with. I have been, and will always be, a battleship sailor.

I remember 16 September 1993, the day that I became a chief petty officer. To have my mom and sister, Susan, pin on my anchors was something that I will always cherish. Being a chief petty officer was not only the highlight of my naval career, but of my life.

And I will remember the *John C. Stennis* for many things, but most importantly, for being ready to fight when her nation called. And fight she did, leaving two months early on deployment, making the world safe not only for your children, but for your children's children.

I have been asked, "What is your favorite memory, John? What are you going to miss?" For me, the answer is simple. I will miss wearing the uniform. There is no profession that garners the respect of the American people more than seeing someone in military uniform.

It has been an honor and a privilege to serve my country. Just like the wrestling team, all I ever wanted was a chance—and for the past 20 years, the Navy has put me on the mat and said, "Go ahead, kid. Let's see what you got."

And you know what? I think we both won.

Epilogue

Challenges and Satisfactions

Well, now that I am leisurely retired, my secret is safely out. Being able to tell people that I have cerebral palsy is a new experience for me, one to which I am still adjusting.

When someone asks, "Why are you limping?" I can now speak the truth. No longer do I have to make up a lame excuse like a twisted ankle, bum knee, or old wrestling injury. I can hold my head up, look people in the eye, and speak freely: I have cerebral palsy.

Most people don't know what to say when I tell them. They just look at me while slowly nodding their heads up and down. Some say, "Well, you look good, I would have never guessed." When I hear that, I think about all those years of physical therapy and silently thank "The Administer of Pain" for pushing my body past the breaking point.

I've also encountered people who almost angrily challenge me with, "You look fine to *me*." I kind of smile and think: sure, maybe when I'm standing still or sleeping! And, while it's true that my cerebral palsy is mild compared to many who are in wheelchairs, unable to care for themselves or even communicate, I too have endured the physical, emotional, and psychological stigma of being "different." I have worked hard, gotten a few lucky breaks, and am proud to have succeeded in my naval career.

It feels wonderful to finally share the truth about my handicap, especially with all the great men and women of the United States

Navy. I must admit, I nervously anticipated the reaction of my shipmates when I first told them about this book. Would they be angry and upset? Would I be treated like an outcast for lying to them for all these years?

I needn't have worried. The response I received from my Navy friends was one of stunned disbelief, "How in the hell were you able to keep this a secret your entire career?" followed almost always by comments such as, "I knew there was *something* wrong with you, but could never figure out what," or, "I thought you had a busted hip that never healed properly and so I never questioned it."

Now they know.

Why did I want to keep my cerebral palsy a secret? When I enlisted, it was prior to the passing of the Americans with Disabilities Act of 1990. I believed I would not be allowed to serve my country due to my cerebral palsy, and I made a conscious decision to lie about it. Whether or not that was the "right" thing to do, I'll leave for others to judge. The ADA was broadened by amendments passed June 25, 2008, which further defines disabling conditions, and specifically addresses the rights of people like me with milder handicaps. On signing the measure, President George W. Bush said, "Let the shameful wall of exclusion finally come tumbling down." It is my sincere hope that this book will assist others in breaking down their personal walls.

I've also met with doctors at the University of Michigan who are doing some great work in their study of CP and aging in adults, one of the first of its kind in the country. A majority of cerebral palsy research is focused on children, which is necessary and useful since that's when the diagnosis and treatment plans are typically made. After my parents found out the facts of my condition from the physicians at Children's Hospital, a multi-disciplinary team approach was drafted with one goal in mind—getting me "up" to a normal level of function. Their hope was that I would one day lead a productive, healthy life. Well, like so many other aging boomers with CP, I have achieved that goal. The next question is—what does the future hold?

To be completely honest, that question scares me simply because I don't know. I have a thousand questions that constantly run through my mind. How long will I be able to safely drive a car? Am I at a higher risk for hip fractures, scoliosis, and arthritis because I have CP? Will my balance continue to get worse? Where do adults with cerebral palsy go to get answers to specific questions such as these? The long-time family doctor? Is the physical therapist at the hospital in my hometown trained specifically to work with adults with CP? There is a genuine need for research and education with programs designed to answer many of these pressing questions. I know the doctors at the University of Michigan are off to a great start, but I believe more needs to be done.

One area for improvement I am particularly interested in is physical fitness geared specifically for adults with CP. I work out in the gym nearly every day of the week, but my workouts have an entirely different focus than most normal exercise routines. For me, it's a form of continued therapy, necessary to maintain and potentially improve function and balance, and to relieve pain. The rubber tubing of my youth has been replaced with a variety of devices including stability balls, wobble boards, and BOSU platforms. These demanding routines challenge my body to keep its balance. The results are stronger core muscles and greatly improved posture. Not being a trained therapist, I am unsure if these are the most appropriate exercises for me. I know my body's needs, but would relish expert assistance to determine if there are any more effective routines or combinations that will improve my functioning, especially as I age. When I discuss my concerns with trainers at the local gym, most give me a blank stare. The internet has not provided much help either. So I just continue with my daily workouts, hoping that I am doing what's best for my body. I'd love to have a targeted workout program designed just for me—an adult with mild cerebral palsy—by an expert in CP research.

With my balance issues and poor depth perception, I have always been nervous about riding a bike, especially in traffic. So for my cardiovascular workout, I go to a spin class twice a week. In addition to burning tons of calories, spinning helps build up my leg muscles and strong leg muscles help maintain a solid center of gravity. It's also easy on my joints and the bike never falls over!

I've tried hiking, but the rocks, boulders, and uneven surface of most trails are too challenging for me. I enjoy walking up Sabino Canyon, a seven mile paved trail in a state park here in Tucson. The scenery is great, and with a smooth asphalt road all the way to the top, it's a nice, easy walk. I know that stretching my stiffened muscles is important, especially as I get older, and walking is a great way to do that. Proper stretching helps alleviate my lower back and nagging hip pain. I've taken yoga classes and seen a vast improvement in my overall health. I look forward to getting back on schedule with those.

Now that I don't fear discovery, I can finally utilize both the medical and alternative fields to help alleviate some of my pain and CP symptoms, which help me function better. I have tried several types of treatment including chiropractic, massage, and hydrotherapy, each helpful in their own way. After avoiding military and civilian doctors for my entire career, I'm finding that's a hard habit to break. I don't currently take any medication for cerebral palsy, although I understand that strides are being made in that important area also.

My military career might be over, but because I have cerebral palsy, I still face unique challenges everyday. I have a hard time standing in one place for very long. My legs twitch when I'm tired at night and occasionally I find myself holding my arms in a unique, frozen pose. And stairs still give me fits. Last year, I attended a Red Wing hockey game with my brother Jim. Our seats were located in the upper bowl of the arena and we had to climb narrow, steep steps to get there. I was fine going up to our section, but descending was another matter altogether. With the game over, the steps were packed with everyone trying to leave at once. After attempting the first step down, I lost my balance and would have fallen if Jim wasn't there to catch me. I had to put my hand on his shoulder as he walked slowly ahead, taking each step one at a time. With the proper blend of diet and exercise, I hope to maintain my independence as I grow older, and not have to rely on others or assistive devices.

But I love to run! I ran the 2000 San Diego Marathon, doggedly sprinting to the finish line in a time of 4:25:47. The kid with cerebral palsy had become a marathoner!

Sometimes, people point their fingers when they see me on long training runs and laugh as I stride clumsily by. I've even had other runners come up beside me during races and ask, "What in the hell is wrong with you?"

I keep going regardless of the insensitive comments. Running with pain, I take it as a personal challenge—how far can I push my body today?

When I competed in the San Diego Half Marathon I had a memorable experience. I wasn't having a good race: every step was more demanding than the one before. I was on the course feeling sorry for myself, just wanting the pain to be over.

Suddenly, this young boy came jogging up on my right and said with a big grin on his face, "Beautiful day for a run, huh?"

I looked down and saw that he had no legs—he was running on prosthetics made from carbon fiber. It was, indeed, a beautiful day for a run.

When I work out, I still get looks and comments. I cannot lift a ton of weight, my feet still slap the floor when I run on the treadmill, and you should see me do an aerobics class! When people approach me now, I use those remarks as an opening to educate people about cerebral palsy, rather than ignore the comments or lie them away.

Mentoring has also proven to be very rewarding, and it's a reward that goes both ways. My friend Phil, now principal of the local middle school, called me not too long ago and requested my assistance with a boy named Trevor, who would be attending the sixth grade. Phil had shared some of my story with Trevor's family and they wanted to meet me. Would I be interested? You bet! So, on the morning of sixth grade orientation, I was introduced to Trevor and his entire family, including his grandparents. I believe it was the first time they had ever met an adult with the same handicap as their boy, someone who had overcome the odds to lead a successful, happy life. We recognized our common symptoms from across the room. My experiences helped educate the family and our relationship continues to support and encourage Trevor. And Trevor continues to inspire me.

I've also been asked, "What are you going to do now?" Writing this book has not only unburdened me but also opened the door for people to talk to me about cerebral palsy, particularly in adulthood. The online social networking site *Facebook* has numerous support groups set up for people that have a friend or relative with CP. It's a great place for anyone looking to share stories, common experiences, and get answers from people actually living with cerebral palsy. I have been able to connect with people from all over the world: London, South Africa, and Australia. With the publication of this book, I hope to get out and meet as many people as I can who've been inspired by my story. I'd love to make it my life's work.

One common theme that I have found in my discussions, especially with the parents of children with CP, is the search for hope. It can be hard to find in this world of absolutes. Medical experts who state with unwavering conviction that "This child will *never*...," teachers who tell parents, "Our testing *confirms* the belief that this child would be better served staying back...," or the coach who dashes the dream of a young athlete by saying, "You just *don't* have what it takes."

Here is a tip for all those people who peddle words such as "never," "cannot," or "certain." Don't tell the thousands of people out there with muscular disorders what they *cannot* do. They've been hearing that for so long that they probably won't listen to you anyway. They are too busy showing you what they *can* do with their lives.

You want an absolute? Here are two:

You are *never* alone.

There is *always* hope.

That's the truth. And it sure feels good to speak it.

History of Assignments of YNCS(SW) John W. Quinn

Assignment	Dates
Recruit Training, Great Lakes IL.	Jan 82 – Mar 82
Yeoman Apprenticeship Training, NTC Meridian, MS	Apr 82 – May 82
USS Point Defiance (LSD 31)	Jun 82 – Mar 83
SEAL Team THREE	Apr 83 – Oct 86
United States Central Command	Nov 86 – Apr 89
USS Iowa (BB 61)	May 89 – Nov 90
USS Chandler (DDG 996)	Jan 91 – Mar 93
Naval Special Warfare Group ONE	Apr 93 – Oct 93
USS Dwight D. Eisenhower (CVN 69)	Nov 93 – Oct 96
Commander, Naval Surface Force U.S. Pacific Fleet	Nov 96 – Oct 00
USS John C. Stennis (CVN 74)	Nov 00 – Oct 02

Index

Photographs are indicated by *ph* following the page number.

style of, 104–105, 123–124
wrestling practice and, 42

San Diego Marathon, 197
sea duty, requirement of, 146
seafarer program, 102
SEALs
  description of, 118–119
  physical training with, 120–121, 123–126
  transfer to, 118–120, 190
  work with, 121–122
shaking, 48, 88, 171–172
shoes, corrective, 21, 21ph, 38–39, 70
shore rotation, Lisa and, 159–160
skating, 37–38, 38ph
skeletal development, 20, 26
sleep, onboard ship, 170–171
smoking, parents and, 56
softball mitt, 137–138
spasticity, 19, 25, 171
sports, 36–38
stairs, difficulty with, 23, 165–167, 196
standing watch, 167–168
suicide, brother's, 138–145
Survivors of Suicide, 142

teasing/harassment. *see also* threats, from co-worker
  awards presentation and, 172
  boot camp and, 91–92
  Driver's Ed and, 48–49
  military entrance examination and, 15–16
  physical fitness testing and, 105
  at school, 20
  SEALs preventing of, 124
  from teammates, 42
threats, from co-worker, 114–116. *see also* teasing/harassment
timed sit, 33, 82

United Cerebral Palsy, 19
USCENTCOM
  assignment to, 131–132
  recollections of, 190
  stress and, 133–134
  transfer from, 145–150
  work with, 132–133
USS Chandler, 155, 158
USS Dwight D. Eisenhower, 165, 171
USS Iowa
  assignment to, 150
  explosion on, 150–153
  photograph of, 154ph
  recollections of, 190
  re-commissioning of, 146
  retirement of, 183
USS John C. Stennis, 165, 187–188, 190
USS Missouri, 146
USS New Jersey, 146, 148
USS Point Defiance
  assignment to, 111–112
  daily life on, 113–114
  experience at sea on, 146, 149
  retirement of, 116
  transfer from, 118
USS Princeton, 190
USS Samuel B. Roberts, 190
USS Wisconsin, 146

walking difficulties, 23–24, 26, 165–167, 171
wandering eye, 20–21, 70
wrestling
  all-area team, 46
  at home, 39–40
  matches, 43–45
  practice, 40–43
  recollections of, 188–189

Yeager, Chuck, 59
yeoman, assignment as, 106–107